1-05-03

P9-DUC-206

Eva,

Let's stand together

in the War on Terrorism,

TERRORISM & OIL

Neal Adams

833

HV
6431
.A22
2003

INFORMATION RESOURCES CENTER
ASIS INTERNATIONAL
1625 PRINCE STREET
ALEXANDRIA, VA 22314
TEL. (703) 519-6200

TERRORISM & OIL

NEAL ADAMS

Copyright© 2003 by
PennWell Corporation
1421 South Sheridan
Tulsa, Oklahoma 74112
800-752-9764
sales@pennwell.com
www.pennwell-store.com
www.pennwell.com

Edited by Marla Patterson
Cover and book design by Clark Bell

Library of Congress Cataloging-in-Publication Data

Adams, Neal.
  Terrorism & oil / Neal Adams.
    p. cm.
Includes index.
  ISBN 0-87814-863-9
  1. Petroleum industry and trade--Political aspects. 2. Petroleum
industry and trade--Political aspects--Arab countries. 3. Petroleum
industry and trade--Political aspects--United States. 4. Energy
industries--Political aspects. 5. Terrorism--Political aspects. 6.
United States--Relations--Arab countries. 7. Arab
countries--Relations--United States. I. Title: Terrorism and oil. II.
Title.
  HD9560.6 .A27 2002
  303.6'25--dc21
                                              2002015747

All rights reserved. No part of this book may be reproduced, stored in a
retrieval system, or transcribed in any form or by any means, electronic or
mechanical, including photocopying and recording, without the prior written permission of the publisher.

Printed in the United States of America

1 2 3 4 5   05 04 03 02 01

DEDICATION

To the girls in my life,
Chris,
Nikeeta, and Holly.

And of course to the other guy in my life,
Pugsley, my cat.

And as always,
to NJA and MJA

PREVIOUS TITLES BY NEAL ADAMS

Well Control Problems and Solutions

Workover Well Control

Drilling Engineering: A Complete Well Planning Handbook

Kicks and Blowout Control

TABLE OF CONTENTS

SECTION I: EDUCATION

SECTION II: ACTION

PREFACE

This book has the single focus of examining terrorism when directed against the oil community. Areas addressed herein include the following:

- Specific terrorist tactics and weapons that have been used against oil and that may be applied in future attacks.

- Attack methods against common oil targets with a description of recognition and handling techniques.

- U.S. and global economic shocks resulting from oil supply disruptions.

- Global and domestic choke points with the potential for major supply disruptions.

- Options to avoid terrorist attacks on oil targets and means to mitigate possible damage.

The text is divided into two sections, *Education* and *Action*, with a goal of serving two distinctly different readerships. If you work within the petroleum industry you may be already familiar with some of the issues of the first section, but the information lays important groundwork for the *Action* topics. Newcomers or those working outside the industry, particularly in government, financial, or service arenas will want to pay close attention to the *Education* points. The topics covered in this book are a concern for every individual in any industry.

Conscientious efforts have been made to avoid lengthy discussions of general terrorism topics and derivates including motivations, general recitation of historical terrorist events, a regrinding of 9/11, Iraq, Islamic fundamentalism, Muslims, Yasser Arafat, Al-Qaeda or Osama bin Ladin. An abundance of available reference sources address the issues, often in excruciating detail. A brief but considered introduction to terrorism has been prepared as a means to develop a level playing field for readers.

A reference list appears at the end of the book. A preponderance of the citations were used in developing more than a single chapter. To avoid the bulkiness of repeating citations in multiple chapters, a compendium approach was taken in creating a single reference listing.

Some readers will invariably differ with the author on issues such as data analyses, assessments, conclusions, and recommendations. The reader's differences are invited and respected.

Public domain resources have been used extensively for research and writing. The U.S. Energy Information Administration and the Department of Defense have websites with an abundance of valuable data and information. CIA analysis and their photographic libraries accessed through the University of Texas online library were beneficial. Original hypotheses established at the initial phase of preparing this book found technical support through these sources. On the one hand, I am thankful for the availability and access to this information, and to the Internet for allowing easy entry to so many research sources. On the other hand, I am troubled because terrorists have the same opportunities.

This book has been written from the perspective of a hands-on engineer tasked with problem solving. Some views expressed are direct and to-the-point. I hope readers will not take offense when considering the world's energy picture is not a bed of roses.

Neal Adams
2002

ACKNOWLEDGMENTS

Leslie Christine Gill Adams was the perfect role model of a wife whose husband writes on occasion. Always supportive, she never complained during periods when I was entranced with work or quasi-comatose after an all-night writing effort. She offered appropriate words of comfort at the needed moment. Chris is my rock.

I have never known a Cyprian fireball until I met Dr. Michael J. Economides early in 2002. His strength of will, intelligence, and unique perspective on most issues elevates him to a level not shared by many. He was the first supporter to share my vision for this book. I hope it meets his expectations.

Nicholas Perez is due credit for graphics development and Internet research on selected topics. His creative genius and relentless work habits resolved seemingly insurmountable hurdles. He will be sorely missed in 2003.

To Ray and Rhonda Perez, the assistance has been invaluable. Rhonda gave a unique perspective as a driven, insightful senior executive at Chase Bank. Ray's Green Beret experiences in demolition were essential in developing an understanding of explosives, sequencing, and detonators.

Michael Burton, member of the Houston Police Department and with Special Forces training, brought everything current about the status of terrorism resistant capabilities in the world's energy capital. Although Michael opened my eyes, I often wish that I were still blind...as ignorance is bliss. Mike, I don't envy your work but I am more comfortable that you and the other Houston Police guys are out there, every day and particularly every night. God Bless You.

This book would have never reached completion but for Marla Patterson and her supporting cast of super-folks at PennWell Publishing. After 30 years of part-time writing, I finally understand the value of a remarkable editor.

FOREWORD

I am the co-author of *The Color Of Oil,* but on September 11, 2001 the color of oil became gray. The optimism that engulfed the United States and much of the rest of the world—and which took two decades to build—suddenly took a dour and sinister hue. Along with the mood, the economic downturn and fear also affected the role that energy and energy abundance played and could play. The royal purple color with which we finished our book a year earlier faded, at least for the foreseeable future.

The quick United States military victory in Afghanistan against a ragtag regime, while perhaps erasing some of the stunned bitterness from the events of September 11, may have little to do with what is in store for the world economy.

The impact on the energy industry and the energy welfare of the world will be enormous and lasting. It is not just the profound changes to economic and social norms of our everyday life that the events will surely bring. Even more important is the intimate connection between the sources of energy and the type of terrorism unleashed with such fury on that fateful day. Saudi Arabia, by far the world's largest producer of petroleum and the home of the most imposing oil and gas reserves, was also the origin of most of the 19 identified hijackers. The rest were from Egypt, also considered a nation friendly to the West. It was ironic, but in retrospect not so curious, that none came from the presumably and officially implacable enemies of the United States—Iraq, Libya, or the Palestinians.

Certainly, the events pointed toward a cultural and social war, accentuated by historical and religious conflicts, the worst possibility of them all. The West and the developed world positively ignored the brewing danger, perhaps due to now-defunct but still lingering colonial superiority complexes, or lack of sensitivity; perhaps due to pervasive disregard of lessons from history, a distinguishing characteristic of a young and vibrant nation such as the United States.

Terrorism, as a means to affect change or to harass the presumed enemy is not new. It is also not new in the oil industry.

Clearly there is a fear that terrorism in the oil industry and trade can exploit geopolitical vulnerabilities and what I would like to call geopolitical choke points. This is a frightening possibility. The Straits of Hormuz, the Straits of Malaca and the Bosporus are extraordinarily narrow and yet enormously busy sea lanes, through which a very sizeable portion of world oil trade passes. The Bosporus in particular, where much exported Russian oil traverses, is less than a half-mile wide at its narrowest point. A large sabotage in any one of these lanes could wreak havoc in the world economy.

However these possibilities are not the only concern. Terrorism in the oil industry, although not necessarily at such grandiose scale, has been pervasive for a very long time. In practically all major petroleum producing countries, socially or politically disgruntled groups have targeted the oil industry through a wide range of terrorist activities as a means to showcase their causes. The fact that local governments draw large proportions of their revenues from oil further exacerbates the situation and renders the oil companies, oil installations, and their employees as very tempting terrorist targets.

It is a tribute to the resilience of the industry and the toughness of its people that they can endure this type of attack, pick themselves up by the proverbial bootstraps, and forge ahead in some of the most inhospitable regions of the world.

My good friend Neal Adams does a masterful job in vividly portraying the terrorist danger against the international oil industry and does it, not in a "crybaby" fashion, but instead in a mature way, fully cognizant of the dangers but also with resolve for an industry whose smooth function is so vital to the welfare of the world and the society as we know it.

Prof. Michael J. Economides
Houston
September 2002

THREE IN A ROW

To the reader: Before you start Chapter 1, I want to share with you a short story. My hope is that you can develop some of the insight on terrorism that I gained from this little experience. You might already agree that, sometimes, the most profound things roll out of the mouths of our younger generation.

Recently, my wife and I were having dinner at a restaurant with family friends and had been discussing my research work on terrorism. While waiting for our meals to be served, our friend's young son, Michael, who had been coloring with the restaurant's toddler give-aways, looked at me and said,

"Mr. Adams, let's play a game. Let's play tic-tac-toe."

I responded as he handed one of his colors to me, "OK, but I'm pretty good at this game", using my best tough-guy whisper. "You move first."

Michael scribbled the tic tac toe box and made the first move with an 'X'.

I playfully glared at him and thought *this might be more difficult than I originally imagined.* I made my move by placing an 'O' opposite Michael's box.

Michael made another 'X',

and then, after exaggerated deliberation, I made my choice.

Michael grinned and said "I'm going to block you and then I'll win," and so he did...or at least so he thought. He made his next selection.

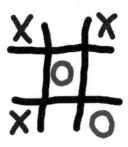

Without hesitating, I inserted my final move.

    With shock in his eyes, he looked up and said "Hey, you can't do that. It's against the rules."

    I silently thought to myself, *That's the essence of terrorism. There are no rules.*

    As a post script, I retracted my move and, as expected, Michael won the game. But in a sense, I won a valuable lesson that may be useful to you during your reading of this book.

SECTION ONE:
EDUCATION

ONE:

WHY OIL TERRORISM—AND WHY SHOULD WE CARE?

So you never bought a book about terrorism. It never seemed to really apply to you. Here's a suggestion. If you live on Planet Earth, your entire lifestyle is based on oil. Terrorism can change every single facet of your way of life. Don't believe it? Read on…

Let's place this discussion in a setting where any person can relate.

Look around you wherever you may be. . . New York, Washington, London, Tokyo, home, your weekend apartment, holiday, late night at the office. As you scan your surroundings, make a mental note of those items in your view.

Make it a game—see if you can identify the oil link to each object you see. Can you imagine any of the following without the critical-path assistance of oil or gas? (Table 1-1)

If you fail to see an oil link to everything within your sight, then congratulations—you're normal. But with trivial exceptions, everything you can see or touch is possible only as a result of the discovery and production of oil or gas. It follows that life, as experienced daily would require substantial restructuring without oil. Some have commented that progress past horse-drawn carriages would not have occurred without it. The merit in this argument seems incontrovertible.

Table 1-1: Various Oil Applications

Obvious Oil Applications	Gasoline for automobiles Airplane fuel Natural gas for home heating Home heating fuel Diesel for 18-wheelers, tractor trailers	
Less Obvious Applications	Automobile/ truck tires All rubber products Soft drinks Condoms Light bulbs Agricultural fertilizers Cassettes, CDs, DVDs Bottle water containers Passport covers Ladies handbags Underwear elastic Tooth paste Hair spray Deodorant Feminine hygiene products Shoes (running, golf, tennis)	Computers and accessories Golf balls Asphalt roads and driveways Water hoses (lawn, car) Ice chests Women's evening dresses Sterile surgical gloves Heart monitoring equipment Pharmaceutical manufacturing Genomics research Plastic notebook dividers Toilet paper Watchbands Construction projects (hydro, nuclear, electric, auto manufacturing)

THE IMPACT OF OIL

"Oil" is used loosely as a collective term that describes items such as:

- liquid oil

- natural gas

- grease

- gasoline

- petrochemicals

But as we can see from Table 1-1, it is the source for many more functions and products than the general public may immediately recognize. Oil products fall into three primary categories—transportation fuel, heating and production fuel, and raw materials.

Transportation fuel. This is clearly the most visible world use of oil product. Oil products, specifically gasoline, diesel, and jet fuel, account for 95% of the transportation fuel throughout the world. By 2020, as developing nations increase their infrastructure energy needs, transportation is expected to account for only 57% of world oil consumption.

Heating and Energy Production. Distillate oils and residual oils provide fuel to heat homes and businesses, as well as to generate electricity and provide power for manufacturing. Heating and energy production accounts for about 26% of refined petroleum use.

Petrochemicals and Raw Materials. Of the remaining oil product use, approximately 13% of refined petroleum is used for raw materials in manufacturing. Most of these become petrochemicals, used in manufacturing thousands of products, including cosmetics, detergents, drugs, fertilizers, insecticides, plastics, synthetic fibers, and hundreds of other products. Other by-products of the petroleum refining process are asphalt, a primary road-building material, and wax, used in a variety of products such as candles and furniture polish.

In addition to the three primary categories, a small percentage of oil use goes to lubrication products, from thin clear oils used in scientific instruments to heavy greases for machinery lubrication.

As mentioned previously, without oil to provide the world's current fuel, material needs, and economies, we would be forced to return to a level of civilization and infrastructure of more than a century ago, at least until suitable replacement fuels and synthetic products can be developed. Those replacements are coming, as new methods of energy production and improved efficiency are in constant development.

According to the *2002 International Energy Outlook*, most of the world's major auto manufacturers plan to introduce some sort of fuel cell or hybrid vehicle by 2010.[1] As these new sources of transportation fuel are created, the world will slowly be able to lessen some of its massive oil dependency. But research indicates that successful commercial application for these sources is unlikely for even an additional decade, due to the economic and logistical issues associated with moving away from traditional gasoline-fueled vehicles.

Therefore, it is likely that the first quarter of the 21st century will see our most intensive dependency on oil as a fuel and materials source. This dependency will increase sharply during the first two decades as developing nations grow toward parity with industrialized nations in economies and fuel/power needs, essentially doubling the world consumption of oil between 1999 and 2020.

In general, our current understanding of terrorism focuses more on direct human attacks, while we have in many cases underplayed the need to identify methods of infrastructure attack that could have much broader and more long-term effect. The world's oil production and delivery system is a critical part of our infrastructure—therefore it becomes a critical piece for examination in planning for potential terrorist attack.

DEFINING TERRORISM

World history, both ancient and current, provides vivid and memorable examples of terrorism in all extremes—from the Spanish Inquisition and New England witch hunts to modern day suicide bombings and high school shootings.

Of course, the most visible and life-altering terrorism example in recent decades is unarguably the September 11, 2001 airliner attacks on New York's World Trade Center and the U. S. Pentagon. It heralded the advent of a new era in warfare, targeting not only government and military entities, but simultaneously attacking civilians as well.

Many experts have attempted to develop a definition for this war against civilians. Governments worldwide have developed definitions that become complex and muddy, as reflected in Title 22 of the U.S. Code, Section 2656 (d):

- The term "terrorism" means premeditated, politically motivated violence perpetrated against noncombatant targets by sub national groups or clandestine agents, usually intended to influence an audience.

- The term "international terrorism" means terrorism involving the territory or the citizens of more than one country.

- The term "terrorist group" means any group that practices, or has significant subgroups that practice, international terrorism.

But for the purposes of this discussion, let's use the *American Heritage Dictionary* version:

Terrorism: The unlawful use or threatened use of force or violence by a person or an organized group against people or property with the intention of intimidating or coercing societies or governments, often for ideological or political reasons.[2]

Actually, the essence of terrorism defies definition. An individual or group attempting to develop a definition lives by a set of rules—expressed, implied or assumed. Civilization developed when rules and boundaries between groups and individuals were initiated. More importantly, the rules were mutually honored, although occasionally honored by forceful means.

Terrorism has no rules and, as such, can't be defined by a society based on rules. Perhaps it's more proper to say that rules of terrorism, for they certainly exist, are in a parallel path with civilization, as they are each a means to an end but have no common elements.

Dr. Jack Welch, recently retired CEO of General Electric, coined the term "boundaryless" as a concept for his business troops to look outside the normally perceived walls of thinking relative to their business lines.[3] He may have inadvertently developed a term that, when applied to this discussion, describes the concept of terrorism in a more encompassing vein.

> *Terrorism: a boundaryless means to frighten*

This phrase is simple to read. It's almost impossible to comprehend.

A HISTORICAL LOOK AT OIL INDUSTRY TERRORISM

Is it far-fetched to deem oil as an instrument of war? The effectiveness of a weapon—any weapon—is evaluated by the same basic questions: *How are the targets affected? Is the damage short-lived or prolonged? What is the economic impact, both from a damage and reconstruction view?*

The history of oil supply disruption as a weapon—used intentionally or otherwise—is a matter of data collection and analysis. But recent disruptions in oil flow have become so commonplace that we no longer consider them a threat. Our complacency has grown because the effect to our economic stride was minimal and acceptable, due to less than severe oil disruptions.

And yet, disruptions have occurred as a result of warfare, and of terrorist activity. The fact that they had minimal impact simply means we've been lucky. . . so far.

As noted in the Preface, this book is not a treatise on general terrorism but rather a focused look at terrorism targeting the oil industry. To start the journey, it is important to understand a brief history of oil-related terrorism events—a few of merit are summarized below. References provided at the end of the book have far more in-depth studies on the history of terrorism warfare for the interested reader.

IRAN-IRAQ WAR

During the Iran-Iraq war of 1980-1988, several oil fields unrelated to either combatant party were the subject of invasion, control, and subsequent damage as combatants retreated to their home territory at the conclusion of the war. The Dorra Field was a victim of these seizures and the damage can only be classified as terrorist-caused since the field and its wells played no role in the conflict.

The Neutral Zone is a small geographical land area located between Kuwait and Saudi Arabia. The region is oil-rich as it covers extensions of the huge Saudi hydrocarbon deposits. Although its land mass is small, its offshore holdings are substantial, both in area and proven oil reserves. Managed by the Japanese-based Arabian Oil Company (AOC), the offshore area has numerous fields including Dorra, located far offshore and falling in an area that, from time to time, is claimed by Iran.

Iran seized all Dorra Field platforms during the war. At the conclusion of the war, Iran retreated to its land territory and returned control of Dorra Field to AOC. Prior to its departure, however, explosive charges were placed on the conductor-casing pipe at the water line and detonated. The conductor and casing were severed. Although the physical damage was considerable, the ultimate effect was minimal as all wells, excepting Dorra 5, had been permanently plugged and abandoned. The No. 5 well is currently static with special equipment placed inside the wellbore at the mudline. (Photo 1-1)

Photo 1-1: Gas platform destroyed in the Iran-Iraq War. Source: Neal Adams Firefighters

This type of damage is common with retreating parties in war zones. A noteworthy example is Saddam Hussein's destruction of the Kuwait oilfields during Iraq's retreat coincident with the Coalition's invasion. Further, as unrest seems to be the event of the day in oilfield regions, this type of terrorism can be anticipated in future conflicts.

1991 GULF WAR

Iraq's 1990 invasion of Kuwait and the resulting 1991 Gulf War is the single, largest overt oil industry terrorist act to the present. Kuwait's oil producing capability, rated at 2 million barrels of oil per day (bopd) in 1990 was effectively destroyed at all levels. (Photos 1-2 and 1-3) After Iraq was driven out of Kuwait, almost a full year was required to extinguish the oil well fires. Subsequent reconstruction of the industry took an additional three years.

Iraq's basis for invading Kuwait was expressed as an effort to reclaim Kuwait as its rightful 19th state, a claim allegedly based in history. Few doubt Iraq's primary but unspoken intent was to expand its oil influence in the region.

From a strategic standpoint and fortuitous to westerners, Hussein's fatal mistake may have been his decision to stop at the southern Kuwait border and not take Saudi Arabia. Iraqi troops took control of the neutral zone between Kuwait and Saudi Arabia and conducted brief operations that suggested their ultimate objective might have been the Kingdom. Even if Saudi Arabia as a whole didn't fall to Hussein, easy control could have been gained over the east while leaving Riyadh to stand.

Photo 1-2: Kuwaiti oil wells set ablaze by Iraq's retreating military forces.
Source: Neal Adams Firefighters

Photo 1-3: Destroyed Iraqi Tanks. Source: Neal Adams Firefighters

For discussion, assume Iraq had taken Saudi Arabia. Oil production capacity under Hussein's direct control would have been overwhelming (Table 1-2).

Also, Qatar would have probably fallen with Saudi Arabia, as it exists on an eastern peninsula jetting into the Persian Gulf with desert at its western back. Qatar has significance with its huge North Field gas producing capacity. This field is the third largest in the world with most of its liquefied natural gas (LNG) production destined for Japan.

Iraq would also have gained control of an additional oil export pipeline. It already owns the northern line running from Iraq to the Port of Ceyhan on the Mediterranean Sea. With Saudi Arabia as a possession,

Table 1-2: Potential Iraqi Oil Control during Gulf War

Millions Barrels (per day)	
Iraq	3.5
Neutral Zone	0.3
Saudi Arabia	11.0
TOTAL	14.8

Iraq would also control the East-West pipeline running to the Red Sea, a pipeline with a 5.0-million bopd capacity.

In a matter of days, Hussein would have wrapped both hands around the world's energy jugular. A crisis of unparalleled magnitude could have ensued if Hussein had chosen to halt oil production. The importance to the western world is that the oil that would have been under his control was bound for western destinations. The feeble stored supplies in the U.S. Strategic Petroleum Reserves would have been consumed before any reasonable military actions could have been taken to reclaim Saudi Arabia. In this scenario, if Hussein had been driven back to Iraq, as was the case with the Kuwait invasion, his scorched earth policy if applied to Saudi would have crippled western economies for years until production could have been restored.

ANTHRAX ATTACK AGAINST AN OIL OPERATOR

The British Petroleum (BP) office in Ho Chi Minh City, Viet Nam was the target of an anthrax attack on October 31, 2001. The bio-agent was found wrapped in a lottery ticket in a meeting room. The building was evacuated and the office remained closed for several days pending confirmation that the white, powdery substance was anthrax.

Testing confirmed the powder was anthrax. A second test by another laboratory verified the results. During this incident, additional letters were mailed to other businesses in the city but none proved to be anthrax.

Staff members became ill from the infection with a few individuals placed in serious condition at local hospitals. The attack did not cause any fatalities. BP and the authorities never received claims of responsibility and the perpetrator(s) were not apprehended.

OIL TERRORISM INCIDENTS, 1999 AND 2000

Table 1-3 demonstrates the global breadth and scope of terrorist attacks against oilfield personnel in 1999 and 2000. It is noteworthy that most entries in the table aren't Middle Eastern in origin.

CAN WE EXPECT MORE OIL ATTACKS?

Will the sun rise tomorrow?

The face of terrorism is evolving at an alarming rate. It is impossible to fully understand the matter before it mutates into a different form. Perseverance seems the only means to get a handle on terrorism so it can be assuaged. But let's not fool ourselves into believing that it will ever go away.

In his book, *The New Jackals*, author Simon Reeve examined the potential growth for terrorist attacks into the 21st century. He relates the story of the Pentagon secret study, 'Terror 2000', for the purpose of preparing the intelligence world for future terrorist threat. According to Reeve,

> The group spent months investigating terrorism and turning its findings into a classified report that shocked the intelligence community. Terror 2000 suggested the terrorist threat was increasing. International terrorists would launch major attacks on the West, it predicted, home-grown terrorists would become a major headache, and—most worryingly—terrorists would increasingly turn to weapons of mass destruction, including chemical and biological agents.

> The report was then presented to representatives from the CIA, FBI, NSA, Defense Intelligence Agency, State Department, and senior officials from the telecommunications, computer and banking industries. It met with a barrage of criticism.

> 'Some of the people thought it was right on—but most of them thought it was too far out,' said [Marvin Cetron, President of Forecasting International]. 'Some of the people said, "My God, how can you believe that, they can't get a hold of these things..."

> ' . . . They thought it was too far-fetched, and that people wouldn't go that far.'[4]

Table 1-3: Recent Terrorist Oilfield Incidents

Country	Date (mm/dd)	Event (year)
		1999
Yemen	01/09	Unidentified assailants abducted a British oil worker.
Yemen	01/31	Tribesmen abducted a British oil worker employed by then-owned Hunt Oil.
Nigeria	02/09	Officials for an unidentified oil company reported that unknown assailants kidnapped two employees, one British and one Italian.
Nigeria	02/14	Officials for Shell oil company reported three armed youths kidnapped one British employee and his young son.
Angola	03/10	Government officials reported an unidentified group kidnapped five oil workers.
Nigeria	06/27	In Port Harcourt, a Shell official reported five heavily armed youths stormed a Shell oil platform, kidnapping one U.S. citizen, one Nigerian national, and one Australian citizen, and causing undetermined damage. The assailants hijacked a helicopter and forced the hostages to fly them to a village near Warri.
Nigeria	07/20	A Shell representative reported armed youths stormed an oil rig in Osoko, detaining 7 British nationals and 57 Nigerian citizens.
Yemen	07/28	In Shabwa Province, armed tribesmen kidnapped a Canadian citizen working on the U.S.-owned Hunt Oil pipeline.
Nigeria	08/10	In the Niger-Delta Region, local press reported armed youths kidnapped three British nationals from a U.S.-operated oil platform.
Colombia	08/26	According to police officials, near Yopal City, police suspected militants abducted a Scottish oil engineer working for the U.S.-UK owned British Petroleum-Amoco Corporation.
Ecuador	09/11	Police officials reported 25 to 30 rebels kidnapped 12 Westerners. Eight hostages, one U.S. citizen, and seven Canadian nationals worked for a U.S.-based oil pipeline company.
Nigeria	10/08	The U.S. Embassy reported armed youths attacked a U.S. oil-company compound housing employees from the United States, United Kingdom, and Nigeria. The attackers injured four U.S. citizens and four Nigerian nationals and caused massive damage to the compound.

Table 1-3 cont'd: Recent Terrorist Oilfield Incidents

Country	Date (mm/dd)	Event (year)
		2000
Colombia	01/29	Revolutionary Armed Forces of Colombia bombed the Cano-Limon pipeline.
Colombia	02/03	In Putumayo, rebels bombed a section of the Cano-Limon pipeline.
Colombia	02/08	Government officials reported guerrillas bombed the ONCESA (Canadian-British-Colombian consortium) oil pipeline near Campo Hermoso.
Nigeria	03/14	Press reported armed youths occupied Shell Oil Company buildings in Lagos and held hostage 30 Nigerian employees and four guards of the Anglo-Dutch-owned company.
Nigeria	04/07	Armed militants kidnapped 40 persons from Elf Aquitaine Oil Company.
Colombia	04/13	A bomb exploded on the Cano-Limon oil pipeline.
Nigeria	04/14	Armed militants kidnapped 19 employees of the Noble Drilling Oil Company.
Indonesia	05/27	Armed militants occupied a Mobil Oil production plant.
Nigeria	02/18	In the Niger Delta region, militants kidnapped 22 Nigerian citizens and 2 unidentified foreign nationals working for Chevron, a U.S.-owned oil company.
Nigeria	06/13	Armed youth stormed two oil drilling rigs, taking 165 persons hostage.
Ecuador	10/12	Militants hijacked a helicopter and took 10 oilworkers.

Time has shown, of course, that the report projections were not only on target, but that the goals of international terrorism groups are truly boundaryless. Even the frightening term, weapons of mass destruction, can no longer be thought of as solely nuclear, chemical, or biological agents. In truth, any tool that can be used to disrupt or destroy the world economies and infrastructure can be as much a weapon of mass destruction as a nuclear bomb.

There is no doubt that terrorists are currently looking closely at every one of these potential tools—including world oil supplies.

CHAPTER REFERENCES

[1] *The American Heritage® Dictionary of the English Language, Fourth Edition*, Houghton Mifflin Company, 2000.

[2] *International Energy Outlook, 2002*, DOE/EIA-0484, U. S. Department of Energy, 2002

[3] Welch, J., *Jack: Straight From the Gut*, Warner Business Books, New York, 2001.

[4] Reeves, Simon, *The New Jackals: Ramzi Yousef, Osama bin Laden and the Future of Terrorism*, Northern University Press, Boston, 1999

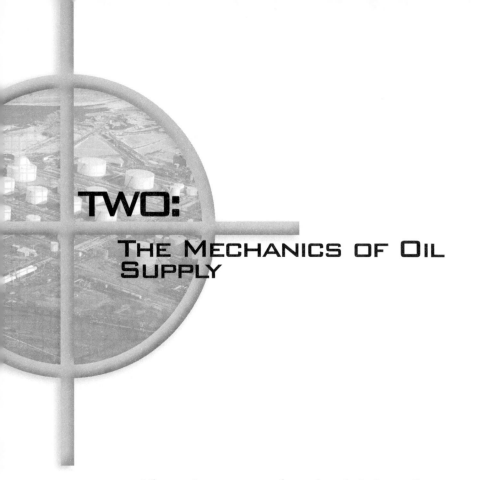

TWO:

THE MECHANICS OF OIL SUPPLY

Oil terrorism can range from the relatively small occurrence of individual well sabotage, which might have more impact on the owner company, to potentially grand scale flow disruptions that could wreak havoc with any country's economy and way of life. Chapters 3 and 4 present overviews of the major disruption issues and their ramifications. But even a single individual with a mind bent on destruction can cause significant consequences.

Author Peter Broussard, in his book, *Energy Security for Industrial Facilities*, relates the 1988 story of a disgruntled ex-employee of a Louisiana oil company who elects to seek his revenge. According to Broussard,

> *What [the worker] did in the course of a single night set off a chain reaction that rippled through the marshes of south Louisiana all the way up to the top stories of the Kayne Building in Houston, the oil company's headquarters. All it cost him was about $248, including a new ax, a cutting torch, acetylene bottle, an oxygen bottle, and some gasoline [to power his boat through the marshland].*

Working under the cover of darkness, he made his way to the oil field, where he totally immobilized all twelve pumping units within five hours. Using only an axe and a cutting torch, he cut through the sucker rod on each assembly so that the entire rod string and downhole pump fell to the bottom of the well. As each unit was disabled, oil production dropped at the field, but the gradual reduction went unnoticed by the production office.

As a finishing touch to his night of destruction, the worker made his way to the oilfield storage tanks, where he left a burning cutting torch to cut through the tank, resulting in a fire and eventual explosion when the acetylene and oxygen bottles were ignited. By the time he had left the scene to reach a safe vantage point,

> *The damage was almost indescribable. Because the oil field was located in a remote area, the fire-fighting capacity needed to extinguish the flames was not on the scene before the fire spread to the adjacent tanks. In all, three 85,000 bbl and one 100,000 bbl tanks succumbed to the initial fire; almost 2 million gal of crude oil were lost.*

And later,

> *. . . putting the production site back together took many months and much capital. The losses in energy went beyond the 2 million or so gal of crude oil and the 500,000 MCF of natural gas that burned. The wells took weeks to repair. The downhole pumps proved stubborn to fish out. But even after they were repaired, they were shut in along with most of the other wells. Crude oil from the remaining storage tanks had to be emptied onto barges to make room for accepting field production from wells that had been shut in for too long. Even with the two tanks empty, field production had to be curtailed.*

Figure 2-1 demonstrates the primary components of oil and gas delivery, and the route from the wellhead to the end-user. Within this route can be seen the most likely targets for terrorist attack: oil and gas wells, storage facilities, transportation systems, refineries, and offshore facilities.

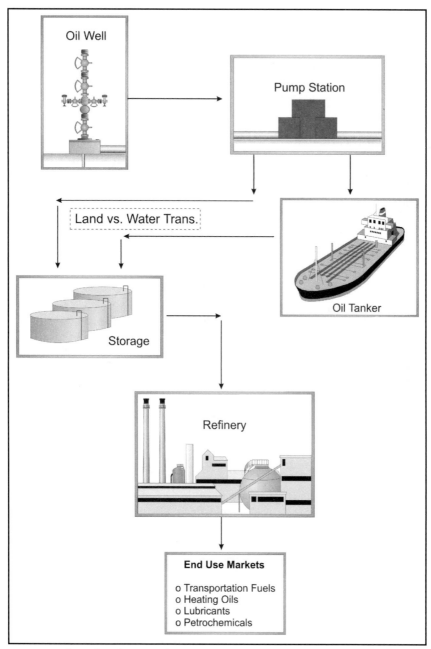

Fig. 2-1: The Oil and Gas Delivery System

OIL AND GAS WELLS

Peter Broussard's story of employee sabotage is an example of the most accessible points for attack in the oil and gas delivery system. There are nearly a million active oil and gas wells in the world, with two-thirds of them located in the United States and Canada. Many can be found in rural areas, along major highways, and in other easy-to-reach areas.

Today, almost all wells are drilling with rotary drilling rigs (Fig. 2-2). The advantage of the rotary rig is that it can drill several hundreds or thousands of feet in one day. These drilling operations are expensive. A shallow well on land may cost $500,000 before it is completed and a deep hole to 20,000 ft can cost upwards of $10 – $15 million, assuming only a few problems are encountered. Offshore wells are significantly more expensive and can easily exceed $100 million for deepwater exploratory wells.

Onshore oil and gas wells could be considered the most vulnerable area of the delivery system, as security for thousands of widely distributed well is almost physically and fiscally impossible. The upside for consumers is that it is also nearly impossible to disrupt enough individual wells in a short period of time to have an impact on the general oil supply. The damage to individual wells will more likely hurt only the well owners responsible for damage repair and lost production.

On the other hand, offshore wells, while far more costly, are by their very nature difficult to access, therefore the security risk is much lower.

STORAGE SITES

The oil and gas delivery system must be dynamic because consumption rates are not uniform. As an example,

- Natural gas usage for home heating is greater in winter than summer and at night compared to day.

- Industrial usage may be daylight–oriented, i.e., 8:00 AM to 5:00 PM or seasonal.

- Gasoline usage is greater in summer than winter.

Oil and gas wells can't be turned on and off as desired to meet consumer demand fluctuations. As such, intermediate storage sites have been developed, generally near the end consumer to meet these needs. These

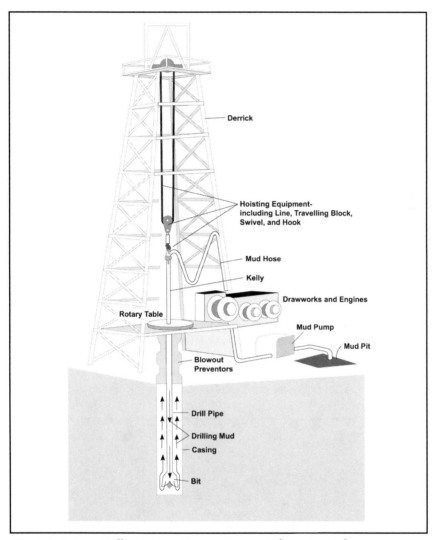

Fig. 2-2: Rotary Drilling System. Source: Energy Information Administration, Office of Oil and Gas

sites may be old wells and reservoirs or specially designed facilities such as leached salt domes. Storage and subsequent withdrawal may be on a daily or seasonal basis.

Arising out of the 1973 Arab Oil Embargo was a U.S. determination to provide some means to mitigate the impact from future disruptions. A plan was developed and implemented to store sufficient quantities of crude to provide a safety net for a specific time interval in the event of future shortages. The storage complex is the Strategic Petroleum Reserve, or SPR.

The Texas/Louisiana region was selected as the general site for the storage complex. This area provided access to incoming import shipments and could easily be connected to the extensive U.S. commercial oil transport network. SPR oil can be easily distributed through interstate pipelines or waterways to about half of the U.S. oil refineries.

The SPR is a U.S. government complex of four storage sites in Texas and the Louisiana Gulf Coast for emergency oil storage. The crude is stored in salt caverns that were either converted or leached for the application. The caverns deep within the massive salt structures offer maximum security at the least cost. The system is 10 times less expensive than above-ground tanks and 20 times less than hard rock mines. This type of fuel storage has been in operation worldwide for many years.

The four complexes include Bryan Mound and Big Hill in Texas and West Hackberry and Bayou Choctaw in south Louisiana. (Fig. 2-3) Multiple caverns exist at each complex with a total of over 50 caverns in the SPR system. A cavern averages a 10 million barrel capacity and can range from 6 to 30 million barrels each. They are generally cylindrical with a diameter of about 200 ft and a height (depth) of 2,000 ft. For comparison, Chicago's Sears Tower can fit inside the average cavern with room to spare.

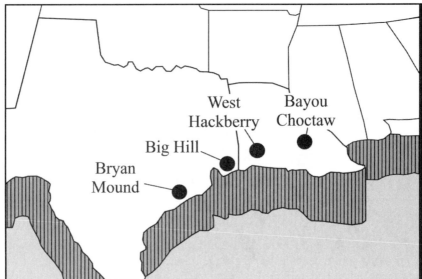

Fig. 2-3: The U.S. Strategic Petroleum Reserve

SPR has required capital and manpower to implement and operate the complex. Investment to date is more than $20 billion which includes $4 billion for facilities and $16 billion for crude. The annual operating budget paid by U.S. workers is about $160 million. Manning requirements are about 125 federal employees and an additional 1025 contractors.

The complex was designed to provide a minimum of 90 days of import protection using public and private stocks. The maximum was 118 days in 1985. However, the increasing domestic demand for crude oil has dwindled the current inventory protection to 53 days. This level is expected to drop at a precipitous rate if the U.S. rate of consumption continues as forecasted.

The maximum drawdown rate is 4.1 million bopd. The expected time for the oil to enter the U.S. market is 15 days from receipt of Presidential orders. The drawdown rate must be compared to import quantities of foreign oil from a single source, which is OPEC in this instance. The 2000 level of imported production was about 6 million bopd and increasing at the present time. If the SPR were called upon to meet an embargo or disruption, a shortage would exist between the usage rate of 6 million bopd and the SPR withdrawal rate of 4.1 million bopd. A backup for the 1.9 million bopd shortfall is non-existent.

The U. S. Strategic Petroleum Reserve has a limited usage history. (Table 2-1) Although the SPR operational periods have been brief, the sys-

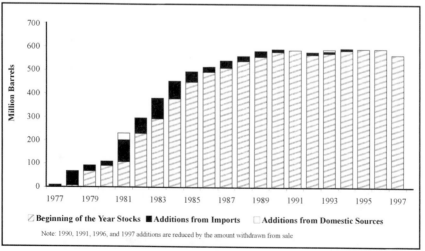

Fig. 2-4: U.S. Strategic Reserves Volume by Year. Source: 1977-1996, Energy Information Administration, Annual Energy Review 1996, DOE/EIA-0384(96); 1997 Energy Information Administration, Petroleum Supply Annual 1997, DOE/EIA-0340(97)

tem is believed capable of pumping its system capacity if required. Inventory as of June, 2002 was 574.7 million barrels with a high of 592 million barrels seen in 1995. Maximum capacity is 700 million barrels. (Fig. 2-4)

Table 2-1: Past SPR Exchanges

Date	Description
May 1996	Exchanged 900,000 barrels of crude with ARCO.
August 1998	Exchanged 11 million barrels of lower quality Maya crude with Mexico.
June 2000	Exchanged 500,000 barrels each with CITGO and Conoco.
Sep-Oct 2000	Exchanged 2.8 million barrels for interim 2 million Northeast heating oil reserve.

The complex was designed to provide a minimum of 90 days of import protection using public and private stocks. The maximum was 118 days in 1985. However, the increasing domestic demand for crude oil has dwindled the current inventory protection to 53 days.

The Clinton administration in 2000 extended the storage concept to include a complex for home heating oil. The action was a result of January, 2000 temperatures in New England plunging to nearly 24% colder than normal which resulted in sharp price increases and a potential stock shortfall. Of the 7.7 million households in the U.S. using heating oil for home applications, about 5.3 million of these households are located in the Northeast and received the brunt of the cold weather.

THE STRATEGIC PETROLEUM RESERVE IS PERHAPS MORE OF A PLACEBO THAN A SOLUTION.

The reserves now contain 2 million barrels of heating oil, which equates to a 10-day supply at average consumption rates. This provides an amount that will allow Northeasterns to become fully aware of the pending disaster before it strikes. The 10-day time period was designed to allow ships to carry heating oil from sources in the Gulf of Mexico to New York Harbor and sites in New England. Storage is at tank farms in Rhode Island, New Jersey and Connecticut.

The Strategic Petroleum Reserve is perhaps more of a placebo than a solution. Quantities of available crude in the Gulf storage complexes and home heating oil in New England are insufficient to meet realistic needs in the event of a severe disruption. In its initial days, the SPR with an inventory protection of more than 100 days provided a small measure of breathing room. At current levels, supplies would be exhausted before any affirmative actions could be formulated and implemented.

OIL AND GAS TRANSPORTATION SYSTEMS

Movements of oil, gas and refined petroleum products require a transportation system capable of handling various fluid types in large quantities. Transfer origins may be at one end of the United States with the delivery point at the opposite end. The primary facilitators in this transportation system are pipeline, rail, road, and water, all of which are extensive in the U.S. The efficient system has developed because of growing distances between origin and market users. Factors influencing transportation decisions include distance, geography, technology and economics.

The initial produced crude oil in the U.S. was bottled in wooden barrels and transported to refineries and ultimately to the market by boat, horse-drawn carriage, or train. These means were to be replaced for the most part by pipelines which first debuted successfully in the 1860s. The initial use for the short sections was connecting producing wells to transport facilities including water and rail. Pipeline distances increased and began to compete with rail, ultimately being declared as the victor in a bitter battle against rail transportation. When technology was developed to allow shipments of more than one product through a line, rail traffic fell further behind pipelines.

Prior to World War II, ships capable of hauling oil, known as *tankers*, were the chief tool used to move petroleum products from the Gulf Coast refineries to east coast markets. When enemy submarines destroyed over 150 tankers during the war, surges in pipelines occurred.

Water transportation gained new life with the era of Alaskan production in the late 1970s. By 1983, water accounted for 51% of domestic petroleum products transportation but would experience a decline to 38% in 1995. Countering the decline experienced by water routes, pipelines accounted for 58% of products transferred in 1995.

Pipelines service most refineries. Trucks are primarily used to deliver the final product from bulk storage to the end user. Rail transportation of hydrocarbon products is small.

The Alyeska pipeline transports Alaska's considerable North Slope production to Valdez for loading to sea-going tankers where its final destination is the U.S. West Coast. Most crude oil shipments within the continental U.S. are via pipeline from the Gulf Coast to Midwest refineries. Tankers and barge movement account for a substantial portion of refined products movement.

Ocean-going oil tankers serve a valuable role in hydrocarbon transportation. Modern design standards include double hulls for protection against rupture and subdivided hulls to allow several types of products to be shipped simultaneously. Supertankers introduced in the 1950s are 1.5 times the size of World War II tankers. The 1960s saw the introduction of VLCCs, very large crude carriers, while the late 1970s witnessed the ULCCs, ultra large crude carriers.

Ocean-going barges are used to transport petroleum products over shorter distances, such as between the Atlantic and Gulf Coast. Their flat bottom design restricts open sea travel and favors calmer shallower waters, typically associated with the Intracoastal waterway systems. Barges handle shipments up the major U.S. river systems such as the Mississippi and Ohio Rivers.

Like tankers, the flat-bottomed barges have subdivided hulls, which serve as tanks, and allows the transport simultaneously of several product types. Individual barge capacity seldom exceeds 30,000 bbl so multiple barges are lashed together for the up-river trip. For the most part, barges are not self-propelled and require one or more tugboats.

Truck tankers handle miniscule amounts of hydrocarbon transfers in the U.S. Their limited capacity prohibits high volume transfers. The advantage provided by trucks, however, is the flexibility of reaching small sites and remote areas.

As the workhorse of the transportation system, the U.S. pipeline grid is extensive. Its objective is to gather oil and gas at individual wells, transport it to refineries for processing to petroleum products and then carry these products to end-user markets. Thousands of miles of pipeline, both large and small, interconnect the system.

Most oil and gas in the Lower 48 State boundaries is produced in the Southwest and Gulf of Mexico. The U.S. population and industries are concentrated in the Midwest and Northeast. To connect the areas, the pipeline grid is heavily concentrated between these areas.

OFFSHORE DRILLING AND PRODUCTION FACILITIES

The offshore oil industry has served a vital role in meeting U.S. and global oil requirements for almost 50 years. Baby steps for the industry were drilling in inland waters or shallow waters near the coastline. A rig used for land operations would be loaded on a barge and then towed to the drill site. Since that time, the level of technology has increased so the current industry has no resemblance to the first pioneers nearly half a century ago.

Onshore drilling methods are the basis for offshore operations with the exception that substantial equipment modifications are required to address harsh marine needs. A large structure is necessary to support the rig over water. As operations move farther offshore and the water depth approaches 10,000 ft, drilling structures must be very sophisticated employing high levels of technology. The vessel design selected for a job is a function of water depth, weather and sea conditions.

Major groups of drilling rigs for offshore work are barges, rigs on fixed platforms, jack-ups, semi-submersibles and drill ships. Barges are used on inland and protected waters where weather conditions are moderate. Fixed platforms set on the seafloor provide a structure for supporting a rig. The fixed platforms are seldom moved and also double as a production platform when the oil and gas wells start flowing. Jackups have legs that can be extended up or down to raise or lower the vessel; these units have a maximum water depth rating of about 300-350 ft, depending on vessel design. Floaters, which are semi-submersibles and drill ships, operate where the water depth outdistances the capability of a jack-ups legs. To date, these vessels have operated in waters to 9,000 ft deep. Each has its own operating characteristics.

Offshore platforms have living quarters for the crew during their work shifts which may range from 7 to 28 days. Personnel facilities include lodging, food, sleeping arrangements, catering crews, and recreational facilities such as TVs and exercise rooms. Transportation for crew members and equipment to offshore rigs is via helicopter, crew boat, or work vessel.

As specialized as offshore drilling has become, the production facilities are even more complex. Designs must address longevity, operations in difficult weather and sea conditions, short term oil storage in some cases, and perhaps provide the ability to accommodate simultaneous drilling or well servicing operations while producing. Current designs are possible due to technological advances and the introduction of high-strength metallurgy (Fig. 2-5).

It should be obvious that these offshore drilling and production facilities are costly. Deepwater facilities can easily surpass the $2 billion price tag. Economic decisions require significant planning and engineering before an oil operator will commit to this level of expenditures. As noted prior, there are no guarantees of success in this risky business.

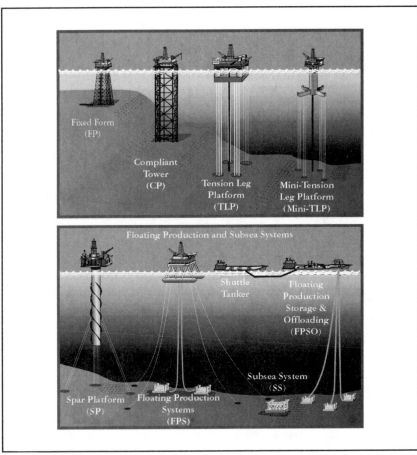

Fig. 2-5: Deepwater development systems. Source: Deepwater Gulf of Mexico 2002: America's Expanding Frontier, MMS 2002

REFINERIES

Refineries are the critical link between produced oil and usable oil products, most importantly gasoline and other transportation fuels.

Oil and gas as naturally produced from subsurface formations is a "crude" mixture of various hydrocarbons, rarely suitable for immediate applications. Most fuel usage mediums such as automobiles, trucks and jet engines are designed to function with a precise formulation of hydrocarbons. The petroleum refining industry provides the processing link between crude oil and/or gas and the finished product and unlocks the ultimate potential of the fuels. As hydrocarbon mixtures have many variations, likewise the refining processes is complicated and contains many steps required to transform crude into usable products for transportation, electric power generation, home heating, industrial applications and a myriad of other uses.

The United States is the historical world leader in refining capability, currently manufacturing about 23-24% of the world's output of petroleum products. An estimated 20% of crude refining capacity is located within the U.S. borders.

As can be imagined due to the gargantuan size of the petroleum industry and the market it serves, likewise petroleum refining is a leader in U.S. manufacturing industries. Refinery production accounts for nearly 4% of all shipments by the U.S. manufacturing sector. The value of shipments in 1996 exceeded $156 billion.

Approximately 45% of refinery output is for automotive gasoline, which is a testament to the mobile nature of American industry and society. The type of refinery product output is varied dependent on demand and has been fluctuating for many years. The 1921 demand was that 27% of crude oil be processed into automotive fuel while the number has risen to 46% in 1996, a high demand period for gasoline.

A typical large refinery costs billions of dollars to build and millions more to maintain and upgrade. It will stay in operation year-round and 24 hours a day, employing 1000 to 2000 people on the average. In addition to the potential hard costs of refinery rebuild and production losses due to an accident or attack, the potential for loss of life due to explosions or gas release is significant. It is easy to imagine the possible ancillary costs in lawsuits should a refinery incident result in damage to surrounding communities.

THREE:

WORLD OIL SUPPLY AND CONSUMPTION

The U.S. Geological Survey, in its most recent assessment of oil's long-term production potential, identified at least 3 trillion barrels (mean estimate) of ultimately recoverable conventional oil worldwide. Because history has shown that only about one-fourth of the oil estimated to be "ultimately recoverable" has actually been produced, rough calculations would place the likely peak in worldwide conventional oil production at some point beyond 2020. —International Energy Outlook 2002

Conflicts in estimates of projected world oil supplies have been a controversy for nearly as long as the industry has existed. It has been a particularly hot topic since the 1970s, in light of oil embargos and environmental/conservation concerns. The pessimistic viewpoint would have the world supply depleted beyond usefulness before 2010. But the best available information in 2002 indicates that technology advances in oil exploration and production will allow for sufficient and affordable world supplies for at least two decades or even more. And history has shown that as we learn more and more about our current reservoirs, even greater resources are located than previously thought. Even as we develop new energy technologies to supplement oil as a fuel, oil will still be a reliable constant for many more years.

In order to understand the dynamics of world oil supply and consumption—as well as its potential for oil-related terrorism—it's important to have a picture of where it's coming from and where it's going. In geopolitical jargon, who controls oil and who doesn't. Here is a rundown of the key countries and organizations in the supply and demand picture.

GLOBAL CONSUMPTION

For the purposes of discussing world energy supply and demand, the countries of the world are divided into six categories, found in Table 3-1. The term industrialized nations actually represents 24 countries scattered around the globe, as referenced in the table footnote. Countries in other groupings can be classified by location due to their proximity to each other.

Table 3-1: World Supply and Demand Arenas

Country Group (ranked by % population)	% World Population (2001)
Industrialized Nations*	18.0
Eastern Europe/FSU	7.0
Developing regions	
Asia	55.0
Africa	10.0
Central & South America	6.0
Middle East	4.0

* Includes Australia, Austria, Belgium, Canada, Denmark, Finland, France, Germany, Greece, Iceland, Ireland, Italy, Japan, Luxembourg, Mexico, the Netherlands, New Zealand, Norway, Portugal, Spain, Sweden, Switzerland, the United Kingdom, and United States.

It is projected that global oil consumption will increase by about 36% between 2000 and 2020 (Table 3-2). Oil has been the primary source of world energy for decades, and is expected to account for 40% of total energy supply through 2020. Other fuel sources, such as natural gas, coal, nuclear, and renewables (hydroelectricity being the most prominent) will continue to grow. However, while those will be increasingly used for power generation, oil will remain the foremost source for transportation, which is expected to grow consistently for the next two decades in both industrialized and developing nations.

Table 3-2: World Oil Consumption Projections

Country	Oil Consumption in MMB/D							Average Annual Percent Change, 1999-2020
	History			Projections				
	1990	1998	1999	2005	2010	2015	2020	
Industrialized Nations	39.0	43.6	44.2	48.1	51.5	54.8	57.8	1.3
EE/FSU	10.0	5.2	5.2	6.7	7.8	9.2	10.1	3.2
Developing Nations	17.0	24.8	25.5	30.4	36.6	43.5	50.7	3.3
Total World	66.0	73.6	74.9	85.2	96.0	107.5	118.6	2.2

Sources: History: Energy Information Administration (EIA), International Energy Annual 1999, DOE/EIA-0219(99) (Washington, DC, February 2001). Projections: EIA, Annual Energy Outlook 2002, DOE-EIA-0383(2002) (Washington, DC, December 2001), Table A21; and World Energy Projection System (2002).

As seen in Tables 3-1 and 3-2, the industrialized nations account for less than 20% of the world's population, but in 1999 consumed 60% of the total world oil produced. While this imbalance has been in play for many years, the picture is gradually beginning to change.

In 1990, developing nations consumed little more than half as much oil as was used by industrialized nations. That gap is projected to narrow by 2020, as the developing nations—particularly Asia and Central/South America—increase their total oil consumption to approximately 90% of the industrialized nations use.

But while the consumption balance between industrialized and developing nations will gradually even out, the production imbalance is and will continue to be overwhelmingly one-sided. While consuming more than 50% of the world oil supply, the industrialized nations currently produce only about 30% of the world oil supply. Out of the top 10 world oil consumers, seven of those countries consume more oil than they produce, ranking highest in net imports (Table 3-3). Italy and Spain are also among the top net importers, consuming 1.7 and 1.5 MMB/D, respectively.

Obviously, the United States—consuming 25% total world oil production—stands head and shoulders above all other countries in comparative oil use. This figure is offset somewhat by the fact that the U. S. also generates 39% of the industrialized nations gross product—a key factor in the world economy. But the news worsens considerably from there.

Table 3-3: Top 10 World Oil Consumers with Net Imports

	Country	Total Oil Consumption (MMB/D)*	Net Imports (MMB/D)
1	United States	19.7	10.8
2	Japan	5.4	5.4
3	China	4.9	1.5
4	Germany	2.8	2.7
5	Russia	2.5	-.-
6	Brazil	2.2	-.-
7	South Korea	2.1	2.1
8	France	2.0	2.0
9	Canada	2.0	-.-
10	India	2.0	1.3

* Includes all countries that consumed more than 2 MMB/D in 2001.

U.S. OIL ADDICTION

The United States was energy independent in the 1940s and 1950s but this changed in ensuing decades. We are now addicted to oil and can't supply enough U.S. oil for our required 'fixes'.

The U.S. is not an oil-rich environment, on a per-capita basis, but does possess sufficient quantities of easily accessible petroleum fuels to serve as a pilot light for a substantial manufacturing base. Perhaps most unfortunate, the U.S. populace has grown to be a society of expectation from an energy view, much like the spoiled rich kid who, given all without question, quickly begins to expect 'everything for nothing'. Sadly, this trend has repeated itself on innumerable occasions during the course of history.

The era of energy independence has faded and will never occur again. In 2001, the U.S. imported 11.6 MMB/D of oil—59% of its total oil consumption—topping several years of record high imports and nearly doubling in volume since 1990. This increasing percentage is lethal. During the early 1980s, U.S. petroleum imports declined from prior levels as a function of economic conditions following the Arab Oil Embargo. The trend began a 1985 reversal and has shown steady import increases until the present time (Fig. 3-1). From the period of 1985 to 1995, an additional 4 million bopd of oil was imported daily. If this trend continues, U.S. oil imports could easily reach 15 million bopd by 2005.

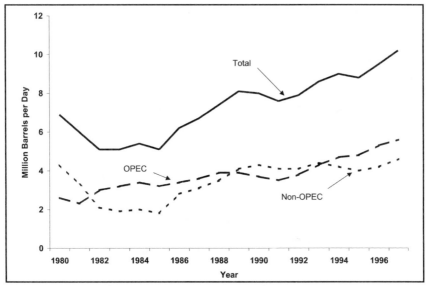

Fig. 3-1: U.S. Petroleum Imports by Source 1980-1997. Source: Energy Information Administration, Petroleum Supply Annual 1997, DOE/EIA-0340(97)/1, and predecessor

The split between OPEC and non-OPEC import sources has been about even since 1980. One source occasionally outdistances the other. These changes are functions of oil price and the coming online of a few major U.S. oil fields such as Alaska's North Slope. From 1992 to 1996, OPEC's share of U.S. imported oil led non-OPEC sources and continued to lead in later years. Reasons include U.S. declining oil production and increasing consumption rate serviceable only by OPEC members.

The western life style is a factor in oil addiction and consumption. The American public seems to be accelerating, both in terms of overall velocity but also in the number of split-second directional changes in daily life. Perhaps to be historically dubbed the 'fast' era, the current American generation knows precious little other than fast.

An analogy is that of the U.S. as a 'Fed-Ex' society that expects satisfaction of needs and desires by 10:00 AM the next day. The public has grown to expect conveniences without an understanding that these expectations run on energy. They started in the 1940s and 1950s when the U.S. was independent of foreign oil and continued when consumption deficits appeared. Oil companies silently bridge the supply deficit by looking to international oil sources such as the Middle East.

This a hard pill to swallow. This assessment is not intended as a condemnation but rather a necessary conclusion, hopefully leading to the development of safe guards against future supply disruptions.

THE WESTERN LIFE STYLE IS A FACTOR IN OIL ADDICTION AND CONSUMPTION

U.S. energy statistics and analyses published by government agencies can be misleading as to a complete picture of oil. They provide a partial understanding of America's history of oil consumption. As an example, the U.S. per capita use of petroleum has declined from a maximum of 31 barrels per person in 1978 to 25 barrels in 1997. (Fig. 3-2) This view is myopic. The 6 barrel decline (31 to 25) sounds encouraging unless one considers a substantial population growth over the same period. The net result is increased daily volume requirements. This must be taken against the backdrop of decreasing domestic oil production.

Energy efficiencies have improved measurably with automobiles, home heating and cooling advancements, and more efficient appliances. MPG ratings on new vehicles have doubled since 1972, even with an average horsepower increase of 63%. Refrigerator efficiencies have tripled. This is good news. But we must remember that Americans own more cars and refrigerators than in 1972.

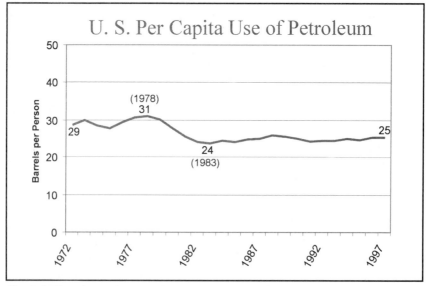

Fig. 3-2: Petroleum consumption per person in U.S., 1972-1997. Source: Energy Information Administration, 25th Anniversary of the 1973 Oil Embargo.

The 1973 Arab Oil Embargo caused a substantial price increase for petroleum (oil), resulting in a partial switch to natural gas where possible, as it is a domestically-produced and lower cost product. U.S. reliance on natural gas has grown such that 67% of new homes being constructed are gas powered. This tendency is crucial as it offsets some of the increasing dependence on foreign oil although the increasing rate of oil consumption far exceeds the switch to natural gas. Dr. Michael Economides, a leading industry expert and co-author of *The Color of Oil*, forcefully advocates a U.S. switch to natural gas where possible. Unfortunately, the transportation industry is not geared to make this fuel switch.

GLOBAL OIL ADDICTION

The U.S. does not stand alone in its addiction to oil. Most global powers are confronted with the same peril. Interestingly, the core countries for industrial strength leads the list of oil users. Since these countries typically are oil importers, industrial footings are shallow at best.

Per capita wealth correlates with per capita oil consumption (Fig. 3-3). The United States leads the list by a sizeable margin. Other notable entries include Japan and Canada. The wealth barometer suggests correlation

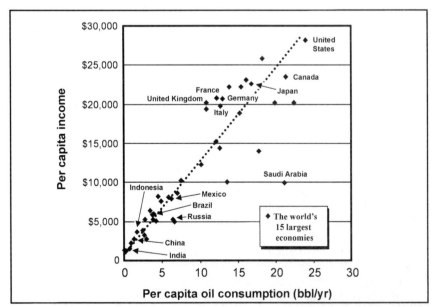

Fig. 3-3: Top 15 World Economies: Per Capita Income in 2000 $ vs. Per Capita Energy Consumption. Source: SPE 77736, Economides, M.J., et al

between affluence and the means to burn extra fuel, i.e., more and larger vehicles, homes and fuel burning appliances.

Quantities of consumed oil are increasing. Table 3-4 shows that during the 10 year period from 1990 to 2000, the U.S. increased its imports by 11% to 18.7 million bopd. In terms of overall consumption, again the U.S. is well in front of the pack. Countries showing the largest percentage increases, such as South Korea and China, are small users from a total quantity view. Their increases are principally due to the ongoing industrialization and growth of the manufacturing base. This analysis shows a growing addiction to oil.

Table 3-4: 1990-2000 Oil Consumption Increases

Major Oil Consuming Nations			
Country	1990	2000	% Change
United States	16.9	18.7	11
Japan	5.3	5.5	4
Russia	5.0	2.5	-50
Germany	2.4	2.8	17
China	2.3	4.8	109
France	1.8	2.0	11
United Kingdom	1.8	1.7	-6
Canada	1.7	1.8	4
India	1.2	2.1	75
South Korea	1.0	2.2	120
* Includes all countries that consumed more than 2 MMB/D in 2001.			

OPEC

The Organization of Petroleum Exporting Countries (OPEC) was established on September 10-14, 1960 in Baghdad, Iraq. Their stated objective is to coordinate and unify petroleum policies among Member Countries, in order to secure fair and stable prices for petroleum producers; an efficient, economic and regular supply of petroleum to consuming nations; and a fair return on capital to those investing in the industry

The founding OPEC members were Iran, Iraq, Saudi Arabia, Kuwait and Venezuela. Six more members, including Qatar, Indonesia, Libya, United Arab Emirates (Abu Dhabi), Algeria, and Nigeria joined between

1961 and 1971. Ecuador joined the Organization in 1973 and left in 1992; Gabon joined in 1975 and left in 1995.

The OPEC nations produced about 45% of the world's daily production in the first quarter of 2002, according to EIA statistics. Of the 73.9 million bopd produced worldwide, OPEC is responsible for about 28.9 million bopd, or nearly 40%. According to 2002 estimates, 80% of the world's proved reserves are located in OPEC member countries.

CARTEL: A COMBINATION OF INDEPENDENT COMMERCIAL OR INDUSTRIAL ENTERPRISES DESIGNED TO LIMIT COMPETITION OR FIX PRICES.

WORLD OIL SOURCES

Given that plenty of oil is available for the foreseeable future, let's examine the location of various known sources.

Table 3-5 is a high impact illustration and a cornerstone of world oil policy. Of the 10 sources shown, six countries and the top five reserves owners are members of the OPEC cartel. Saudi Arabia's estimated crude reserves are greater than Iraq and United Arab Emirates combined. The top four are located in the Middle East contiguous to the Persian Gulf. OPEC acts as a monopoly, has done so in the past and will undoubtedly continue to stroke their monopolistic powers in the future.

Table 3-5: Top World Oil Reserves *(includes all countries exceeding 5 billion barrels)*

	Country *(Italics represent OPEC members)*	Estimated Reserves 2002 (1000 bbl)
1	*Saudi Arabia*	259,000,000
2	*Iraq*	112,500,000
3	*United Arab Emirates*	97,800,000
4	*Iran*	89,700,000
5	*Venezuela*	77,685,000
6	Russia	48,573,000**
7	Mexico	26,941,000
8	*Nigeria*	24,000,000
9	United States	22,045,000
10	Norway	9,447,290

** Represents a combination of estimated and probable reserves.

Russia doesn't rank high on the estimated reserves scale. However, it is important to note that Russia has huge regions falling into the probable reserves category, which accounts for its sixth place ranking in the reserves list. If these areas can be upgraded to proven reserves as Russia's oil industry restructures itself, they should move much higher on the list. Much of Russia's reserves are in the remote Siberian region with its harsh weather conditions and poor infrastructure required to support a burgeoning oil industry.

Prior to the 1973 Arab Oil Embargo, the United States imported large quantities of oil, principally from Saudi Arabia and Iran, both considered allies before the disruption. Subsequent to the Embargo, the United States began to move away from Middle Eastern sources in favor of Western Hemisphere countries, most notably Venezuela, Mexico and Canada. This policy was strategically sound, although it is not an absolute cure.

Only a handful of giant oil fields exist in the world and they account for most of the world's reserves. In 1984, there were 265 world-scale "giant" oil fields, 18 of which had 10 billion barrels or more of recoverable resources. Saudi Arabia has the world's largest known oil field, the Ghawar Field, which was discovered in 1948. Ultimate resources of this field are estimated at 123 billion barrels of recoverable crude oil, of which 48.9 billion barrels have already been produced.

Table 3-6: Top World Oil Producers 2001 (includes all countries producing 2 MMB/D or more)

	Country (*Italics represent OPEC members*)	Total Oil Production 2000 (1000 bbl)
1	Saudi Arabia	9,145
2	United States	7,745
3	Russia	6,535
4	Iran	3,770
5	Mexico	3,450
6	Norway	3,365
7	China	3,245
8	Venezuela	3,235
9	Canada	2,710
10	Iraq	2,635
11	United Kingdom	2,660
12	United Arab Emirates	2,515
13	Nigeria	2,105

Table 3-6 describes daily oil production rates for OPEC and non-OPEC countries. On top of the list is Saudi Arabia, and Iran, Venezuela, Iraq, the United Arab Emirates, and Nigeria also rank in the top producers category as well as the top reserves.

U.S. PETROLEUM RESERVES

OIL

At the end of 1997, the United States had an estimated 22.5 billion barrels of proved crude oil reserves and 8.0 billion barrels of proved natural gas liquids reserves. Most are located in Texas, Alaska and California, which mean the U.S. oil industry is divided between opposite ends of the country. Texas had an estimated 5.7 billion barrels and Alaska had an estimated 5.2 billion barrels of crude oil proved reserves at the close of 1997. California had 3.8 billion barrels. Offshore areas of California, Texas and Louisiana contain large proved reserves. A total of 2.7 billion of the 3.5 billion barrel total were in federally controlled offshore waters, known as the Outer Continental Shelf (OCS).

The Prudhoe Bay Field on the north slope of Alaska is the largest field discovered in the United States. Discovered in 1960s, its ultimate recoverable resources are estimated at 13 billion barrels. Its remaining proved reserves were estimated to be 3.3 billion barrels in 1999. Production rates from Prudhoe Bay are declining rapidly as the field moves past its maturity. The second largest U.S. field is located in East Texas and was discovered 60 years ago. It has only 1 billion remaining of its original 6 billion barrels.

Another field exists on the northern slope of Alaska in the Alaska National Wildlife Refuge (ANWR). Its reserves are believed to be comparable to Prudhoe Bay when it was originally discovered. Drilling on the barren rocky wastelands has been stymied in Congress even though actively supported by President George W. Bush. Its future is uncertain.

Most U.S. resources have been previously developed. Other areas in the world hold more promise for economic discoveries. Remaining recoverable crude oil in the U.S. is about 3% of the world's total. The prospect of finding major new discoveries is diminishing. The U.S. had 3.2 billion barrels of indicated additional crude oil reserves at the end of 1997, which are subject to reclassification later.

Outer Continental Shelf regions account for nearly 25% of U.S. crude production, or 1.6 million bopd, which is the highest level since 1973. This peak percentage is misleading, however, as its percentage rise is due to the decline in Alaska production.

Estimates for undiscovered resources are vague but range up to 77.9 billion barrels of undiscovered technically recoverable oil. About 60% of these resources are located far offshore in the Outer Continental Shelf where finding costs may be 100 times greater than equivalent land wells.

GAS

U.S. gas sources generally parallel oil producing regions. Most domestically produced natural gas originates in the offshore Gulf of Mexico (GOM). It is piped to end markets with almost 50% of the gas destined for the Northeast and Midwest. Chapter 6 contains maps indicating gas pipeline routes from source to end markets in the U.S.

The GOM is the dominant source for domestic natural gas. It accounts for 30% of natural gas production and 20% of proved reserves. Its production may be supplemented from Alaska's North Slope if appropriate pipelines are constructed.

Total natural gas production in the Lower 48 States has shown an upward trend in the 1990s and continuing into the new millennium. The rate in 1990 was 47.7 Bcf per day or an annualized volume of 17.4 Tcf. It climbed to 54 Bcf per day, or 19.8 Tcf per year in 2000. These rates are averaged since daily production rates are not constant throughout the year.

Canada is becoming a key production player for U.S. natural gas supplies. The Canadian import capacity to the U.S. is approximately 4.5 Bcf or 8.3% of the average daily U.S. consumption in 2000. Imports should continue as Canada is working hard to find markets for their gas produced in western Canada, most of which is from Alberta. East Coast Canadian sources such as Sable Island off the coast of Nova Scotia also should provide gas to the U.S. when production facilities come on line.

A concerted effort is ongoing to switch America's energy sources from crude oil to natural gas. The critical necessity for the conversion became prominent as a result of the 1973 Arab Oil Embargo. Natural gas offers the important advantage that it is produced within the United States in plentiful supplies. This gives America more control over its own destiny with respect to fuel supply.

However, this solution is not a complete energy remedy. As shown in Figure 3-4, approximately 12.1 MMB/D (or 65%) of crude oil usage goes to transportation. This market can't be switched completely to natural gas, particularly in the foreseeable future. However, an energy supply burden is lightened each time natural gas finds an avenue to replace crude oil.

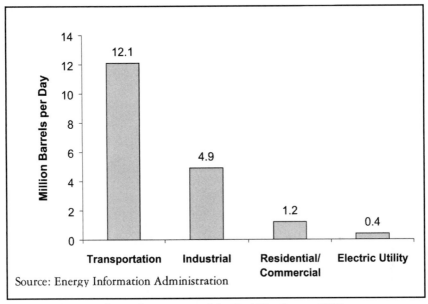

Source: Energy Information Administration

Fig. 3-4: Estimated Petroleum Demand by End-Use Sector, 1997
Source: Energy Information Administration, Annual Energy Review 1997,
DOE/EIA-0384.

OIL TRAFFIC ROUTES

The traffic routes to end market users are equally as important as the size and locale of oil deposits. Figure 3-5 illustrates these routes with each path scaled to indicate daily transit volumes.

The immediate lesson from this illustration is the highly disproportionate amount of daily oil volume produced from the Middle East as compared to other global producers. Data on the figure shows 883 million tons/year flows from the Middle East contrasted with 123 million tons from Russia and 132 million tons from Venezuela. This type of imbalance creates potential instability issues.

Annual supplies to the United States show little dependence on Middle East oil. Current sources are Venezuela (132 million tons), Mexico (89 million tons), Canada (73 million tons), North Sea (53 million tons) and remaining imports from Nigeria and the Middle East. This picture has changed substantially since 1973.

Japan is in a difficult position due to a lack of domestic hydrocarbon deposits. It imports nearly all its energy supplies. The scaled arrow indicates substantial import volumes. Japan has worked hard for many years to forge alliances with oil suppliers as a means to solidify relationships. They have made heavy financial investments in countries such as Qatar to build fertilizer plants and petroleum-related projects. However, Japan is confronted with the same reality as other importers because price shocks from oil disruptions will affect all users equally.

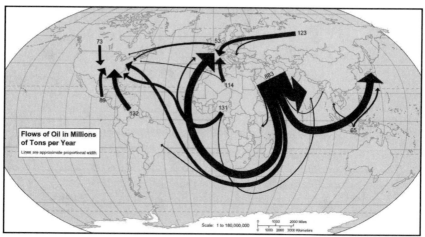

Fig. 3-5: Global Oil Traffic. Source: Energy Information Administration

PRODUCTION AND UNUSED CAPACITY

In Table 3-6, developed by the EIA, note the columns for 'Production Capacity' and 'Unused Capacity'. The unused capacity is the difference between the production capacity and the estimated (daily) production.

This example shows that Saudi Arabia has the ability to produce an additional 2.8 million bopd in excess of its current production estimated 8.2 million bopd, if events should require it. The sum of unused capacities for the data in Table 3-6 is 6.3 million bopd on a world basis.

Unused capacity is considered a safe haven for troubled oil times. Should one oil source experience a disruption, i.e., mechanical issues, terrorism, civil war etc, another source(s) could step up and cover shortfalls.

Table 3-6: First Quarter 2000 Oil Production[1] and Capacity[1] Estimates

	Production Capacity	Estimated Production	Unused Capacity
OPEC			
Saudi Arabia[2]	11.0	8.2	2.8
Iran	3.9	3.6	0.3
Kuwait$_2$	2.6	1.8	0.8
United Arab Emirates	2.8	2.3	0.5
Other Persian Gulf	3.8	3.7	0.1
Persian Gulf OPEC	24.1	19.6	4.5
Venezuela	3.3	3.0	0.3
Nigeria	2.4	2.0	0.4
Other Non-Persian Gulf	4.6	4.3	0.3
Non-Persian Gulf OPEC	10.3	9.3	1.0
Total OPEC	34.4	28.9	5.5
Non-OPEC			
United States	9.1	9.1	0.0
North Sea	6.9	6.7	0.2
Other OECD	4.3	4.3	0.0
Total OECD	20.2	20.0	0.2
Former Soviet Union	7.4	7.4	0.0
Mexico	3.7	3.3	0.4
Other Non-OECD	14.6	14.4	0.2
Total Non-OECD	25.7	25.0	0.6
Total Non-OPEC	45.9	45.0	0.8
Total World	80.2	73.9	6.3

Source: EIA
[1]Estimates include crude oil, natural gas liquids, other liquids, and refinery gain.
[2]Saudi Arabia and Kuwait do not include the Neutral Zone, which is in "Other Persian Gulf".
Iraq's unused oil production capacity is assumed to be zero, as its production is constrained by United Nations sanctions.
Also, totals may not add due to independent rounding.

But these factors might not be as reliable as first perceived. Consider a not-too-far-fetched example and you be the judge.

Fact: Iran seized three key islands in the Straits of Hormuz in 1992. The islands are the Greater Tunb, Abu Masa and the Lesser Tunb. Construction projects are underway on these islands.

Fiction: *The long-range gunnery installations, according to NSA satellite imagery, appear to be directed towards the 2-mile wide outbound shipping lane exiting the Persian Gulf. Iran has declared that outbound oil traffic headed for Western sources will be destroyed if attempting to pass through the Strait of Hormuz. In a sympathetic move, Iraq has announced it will shut off oil supplies if attacks are made on Iran.*

Fact: The Strait of Hormuz conducts about 14.5 million bopd bound for Japan, United States and Western Europe. If the Strait is closed, the sole alternative for oil transport is the Saudi Arabian East-West pipeline to the port of Yanbu on the Red Sea. The East-West pipeline has a capacity of about 5 million bopd with a current utilization of about 2 million bopd. This leaves about 3 million bopd of unused pipeline flow capacity.

Considering that 14.5 million bopd could be affected by the Strait closure and that an additional 3 million bopd can be pipelined to the Red Sea, a 12.5 million bopd deficit in meeting world demand cannot be satisfied with unused capacity or alternate sources.

If Iraq were to halt its oil flow in conjunction with Iran's actions, the deficit is increased to 14.5 million bopd.

Unused worldwide production capacity is not a safe harbor as widely considered, nor does it provide any relief if the base daily production cannot be delivered. Saudi Arabia's unused capacity of 2.8 million bopd is meaningless if their base production level of 8.2 million bopd cannot be delivered.

Assuming we dismiss this possibility in the Strait of Hormuz, consider an environmentalist attack on a nuclear-laden tanker while passing through the Bosporus Straits destined for Russia's new dumping grounds. Or an anti-Mubarak faction attacking the Suez Canal-Sumed pipeline complex in protest against Egypt's dependence on western aid. Let's not forget the Panama Canal/pipeline or the Malacca Strait or the Spratly Islands or Alyeska. The issue causes concern because of each route's importance and that it generally requires transit through troublesome regions.

SUMMARY

This volume of production and consumption information underscores the delicate balance of world oil supply in today's political and economic arena. Our world interdependence is heavily established and will not change without massive changes within individual countries. Particularly in the United States, we don't allow for the possibility of a major supply disturbance. But a variance of even 2 MMB/D could instigate escalating oil prices and a global economic imbalance. If a group intent on attack hits one major choke point plus a few easy U. S. targets, our lives will change quickly and dramatically for the worse with no hope of recovery in the near future.

Don't think that the current international terrorist factions are unaware of this information and it's implications. Information arising in the aftermath of the 9-11

> OUR WORLD INTERDEPENDENCE IS HEAVILY ESTABLISHED AND WILL NOT CHANGE WITHOUT MASSIVE CHANGES WITHIN INDIVIDUAL COUNTRIES.

attacks has already proven their ability to manipulate stocks, financial resources, and information resources to support their plans. In all likelihood, they are much more aware of the potential damage through disruption than most citizens and many government officials.

FOUR:

OIL AS A WEAPON

Not if. . . but when!

In the 2002 world climate, terrorism evokes images of immediate destruction. The western world has acclimated rapidly to the idea that a terrorist can use a device of violence—or even a chemical or disease dispersion—to disrupt lives in a matter of seconds, hours, or days.

But what if the attack were made in a more subtle and long-lasting method—one that could sap civilization's lifeblood. Impossible...you might think!

DISRUPTIONS

Disturbances in the world oil flow are referred to as disruptions. Historically, they have stressed the world economy, even though past incidents have been restrained and less warlike than could have occurred. Under adversarial conditions, the outcome could have effected a deeper and much more damaging impact.

Consider the three larger disruptions, beginning with the 1973 Arab Oil Embargo. OPEC announced an oil boycott against countries that aided Israel during the "October War" (Table 4-1). OPEC's crude oil production was reduced by 4.2 million bopd, although the global effect was offset slightly by increased production from the U.K. and Norway. World oil prices doubled between October 1973 and January 1974.

Table 4-1: *Global Oil Supply Disruptions Since 1951*

Date	Duration (mths)	Volume (million/ bbl/d)	Reasons
Mar 1951-Oct 1954	44	0.7	Iranian oil fields nationalized following months of unrest and strikes
Nov 1956-Mar 1957	4	2.0	Suez War
Dec 1966-Mar 1967	3	0.7	Syrian transit fee dispute
Jun 1967-Aug 1967	2	2.0	Six Day War
May 1970-Jan 1971	9	1.3	Libyan price controversy, damage to Tapline
Apr 1971-Aug 1971	5	0.6	Algerian-French nationalization struggle
Mar 1973-May 1973	2	0.5	Unrest in Lebanon, damage to transit facilities
Oct 1973-Mar 1974	6	2.6	October Arab-Israeli War, Arab Oil Embargo
Apr 1976-May 1976	2	0.3	Civil war in Lebanon, disruption to Iraqi export
May 1977	1	0.7	Damage to Saudi oil field
Nov 1978-Apr 1979	6	3.5	Iranian revolution
Oct 1980-Dec 1980	3	3.3	Outbreak of Iran-Iraq War
Aug 1990-Oct 1990	3	4.6	Iraqi invasion of Kuwait
Apr 1999-Mar 2000	12	3.3	OPEC cuts production to increase oil prices

Iran and Iraq were in a heated battle for a number of years. At its beginning of the war in 1979-1980, a 5.4 million bopd loss of production occurred which represented 9% of world oil production. Supplies from other oil sources could not fill the void. The price of oil doubled again.

Iraq invaded Kuwait in 1990. From May to December 1990 total oil output fell by 4.8 million bopd, or 7.6% of world production. The result was another price doubling, from $17.50 to $33 per barrel (1993 prices).

In the three cases described here, OPEC members maintained a relatively constant production level, which left the world oil market at a deficit from prior levels.

These disruptions came at a large price tag to Americans. Cost estimates from 1972 to 1991 are $4 trillion (1993$). In addition to monetary losses, the cost of disruptions included,

1) a reduction in economic output due to restrained resources,

2) sudden and drastic changes in energy costs, causing layoffs when output product prices could not adjust quickly enough to support wages, and

3) the wealth of U.S. citizens transferred to OPEC members and were never recovered.

The effect of disruption-caused oil price increases on U.S. gross domestic product (GDP), is clearly seen in Figure 4-1.

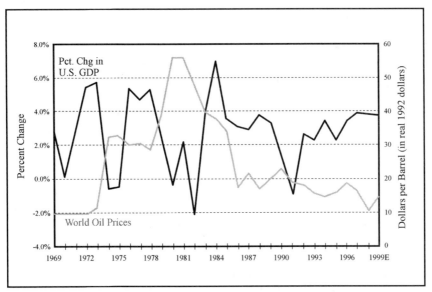

Fig. 4-1: Oil prices adversely affects U.S. Gross Domestic Product. *Source: Energy Information Administration, Oil Price Impacts on the U.S. Economy, January, 2000.*

To discern a range for oil price shocks from future disruptions, the U.S. Department of Energy has run simulations for several disruption scenarios. They studied supply drops of 1, 3, and 6 million bopd, which were considered as low, medium, and high risk prospects. Price increases for the three net disruption sizes were $3.70, $11 and $32 per barrel above the base price existing prior to the disruption. It should be remembered from Table 15.2 that major disruptions have been in the 3-6 million bopd range with a tendency to approach the upper limit.

As a result of the 1973 Arab Oil Embargo, the U.S. has shifted the majority of its imports from Middle Eastern sources to Venezuela and Mexico. On first inspection, this might suggest a reduced vulnerability to disruptions in Middle Eastern oil traffic. But this view does not provide a true situational analysis.

A major disruption will cause global price escalations, regardless of its origin. If a disruption occurred in Venezuela, however, the effect would be two-pronged due to a deficit import flow to the U.S. in addition to the price increase. The net effect of this scenario is much greater than the price differential because, as history has shown, a GDP and employment drop would be expected.

An analysis of present-day oil flow events fails to reassure western powers. In isolation, consider only Iraq's May-June 2002 threats of an oil embargo, which would have amounted to 2 million bopd. Had Mr. Hussein gone forth with his threats, oil price destabilization accompanied by the U.S.'s fluctuating industrial base would have aggravated the economic depression occurring at the time.

A MAJOR DISRUPTION WILL CAUSE GLOBAL PRICE ESCALATIONS, REGARDLESS OF ITS ORIGIN.

Future oil disruptions seem inevitable. Terrorists, particularly those in the fashion of Al-Qaeda and other fundamentalist groups, are knowledgeable, inventive, resourceful, and have proven to be capable of sustaining a pace two steps ahead of western intelligence and law enforcement agencies. Substantial oil disruptions, as described in a hypothetical setting in other sections of this work, appear to be a matter of time as opposed to probability.

The 1973 Arab Oil Embargo caused a substantial price increase for petroleum (oil), resulting in a partial switch to natural gas where possible, as it is a domestically-produced and lower cost product. U.S. reliance on natural gas has grown such that 67% of new homes being constructed are gas powered. This tendency is crucial as it offsets some of the increasing dependence on foreign oil although the increasing rate of oil consumption far exceeds the switch to natural gas. Unfortunately, the transportation industry is not geared to make this fuel switch.

Oil Cost. The per barrel price paid for imported and domestic oil is about $20-30/bbl depending on the economic swing cycle. Oil's ultimate cost has implications other than simple monetary exchanges.

How would it affect everyday life if oil supplies were suddenly curtailed? Gasoline prices will increase, perhaps by as much as 100%. Unfortunately, this gasoline price increase is underestimated and only the iceberg tip.

The oil price ($/bbl) is an OPEC price-fixed value, not a floating market variable. The price is overtly fixed, pending acceptance of member countries and their respective production quotas, and seems to be maintained in a range allowing reasonable world GDP expansion.

What does this mean relative to oil price? Imagine a balloon that floats, high or low, while remembering that—regardless of its elevation—the balloon is only filled with air. By comparison, the price of oil floats without a substantive basis. OPEC is unrestrained in establishing most price limits. Oil could trade from a low of $8-10/bbl to as much as $100-$200/bbl. The practical upper limit approaches a level causing curtailment of industrial activity but less than an amount causing actionable world unrest. Since the 1970s, OPEC has manipulated production and price at its discretion but always within a range that allows continued economic growth.

Suppose there were a case where oil flow is suddenly closed through the Strait of Hormuz. The supply side of the equation would be short by about 14.5 million bopd, a deficit that couldn't be resolved with global unused capacity. The short-term result is items such as gasoline, air conditioning, and ice for your drinks would not be available, regardless of the cash available to pay for the items.

If oil were suddenly disrupted to such a degree, the require changes would be life-altering. Transportation is a major end-user for oil products, consuming about 53% of total world oil consumption and growing annually. (Fig. 4-2) The trucking industry would be hurt, causing substantial price changes in goods normally transported by this means. This includes food, clothing, medicine and most other products used daily by the population. The U. S. airline industry would be severely affected and could easily become insolvent, considering its 2002 fiscal condition. Vacations and week-end trips with low gas mileage vehicles may become history. The percentage used by the industrial community for producing goods would require rationing.

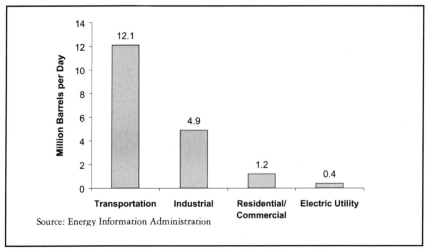

Fig. 4-2: Estimated Petroleum Demand by End-Use Sector, 1997. Source: Energy Information Administration, Annual Energy Review 1997, DOE/EIA-0384.

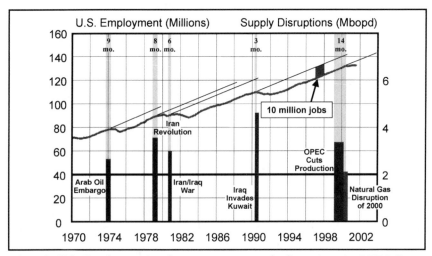

Fig. 4-3: U.S. Employment and major energy supply disruptions in OPEC Era. Source: Energy Information Administration and U.S. Dept. of Labor, assembled by Longbottom and Oligney (SPE77371)

Figure 4-3 demonstrates the severe impact of previous oil disruptions and the price paid by Americans. Since 1970, the U.S. (and the world) has experienced five major oil disruptions, all due to Middle Eastern causes. The duration of the disruption has ranged from 3 months with the Iraqi invasion of Kuwait to 14 months during the 1998-1999 OPEC production cuts.

Focus on U.S. employment and its reaction following each disruption. In every case, available jobs have declined substantially, presumably due to adverse affects on employers. People lost their jobs and couldn't find other employment in many cases.

Another point relating to jobs must be considered. Job growth preceding each disruption was increasing. If the trend would have continued without disruption, analysis suggests that the 2002-2003 job market should be much larger. As an example, if the trend from 1984 to 1990 were to have continued, about 10 million additional jobs would have been created. For convenience, trend lines are shown for each period prior to a disruption and then continued forward.

An important issue must be clarified relative to the disruption and its effect on U.S. employment. In each of the five cases, the disruption was not as severe as it could have been had OPEC made a concerted effort to halt 100% of their oil flow to western users rather than simply retard them. If a complete disruption were to occur, its overall effect is almost too unimaginable to assess.

SIEGE WARFARE

An effective and time-proven tactic in the arsenal of military options, siege warfare has been abandoned by most present-day political and military entities as a time-consuming technique that has outlived its usefulness. Used to deny life-sustaining needs such as food, water, and supplies, siege techniques were directed at fixed enemy stalwarts, usually castles.

Inside the castle, the defending forces were seldom concerned about a specific attack due to protection from high walls. Their focus instead turned to mustering a fighting force after long periods of siege warfare. To prepare for the endurance struggle, inhabitants stockpiled large quantities of food and munitions. The final outcome was determined by the attacker's persistence vs. the quantity of reserves stored in the castle prior to the siege.

Perhaps siege warfare is past its prime as a conventional military weapon, but in an era where decidedly unconventional warfare is at hand, anything could happen. And the components are certainly in place to reconsider its potential.

Consider a few basics associated with siege warfare:

- The attacker has the flexibility to choose circumstances upon which the siege will be conducted.

- After starting the siege, the attacker has great freedom of action or inaction.

- The attacker's primary concern is to safeguard against an opponent's sudden and unexpected offensive move.

- Significant supplies must have been placed in reserve in anticipation of the siege if the defender has hopes of surviving the contest.

History shows most defendants' downfall in siege warfare is the lack of preplanning and storing sufficient materials to maintain an effective fighting force.

Let's evaluate the applicability of these warfare basics if oil is used as a weapon.

- Middle Eastern supply sources and terrorists choose the time and place.

- Oil users are without supply alternatives.

- Oil suppliers control the manner they choose to prosecute the war.

- Western importers as the primary oil users have not prepared for this type of attack.

- Oil stockpiles are virtually non-existent.

- Importers may be unable to mount a major counter-attack due to fuel shortages.

Have you ever heard of the Golden Rule? He rules who has the Gold!
Same thing with oil, but the color is black...hence the name black gold.

In 2002 the United States and other western importers are unprepared.
Key issues underlying this weakness are unlikely to change until forced by
such an event.

- The U.S. is addicted to oil in gluttonous amounts.

- The addiction is becoming more severe.

- Alternative fuel sources such as coal, nuclear energy, and fuel cell
  technologies exist but can't be martialed in a realistic time frame.

- Fuel conservation is poor.

- Energy stockpiles for the U. S. and other importers are inadequate
  to cover basic society requirements beyond several weeks.

- The U.S. is self-restricted from increasing its own oil supplies
  through new exploration and production.

- Systems aren't in place to handle this emergency, i.e., emergency
  rationing guidelines, industry shut-down sequencing or conservation measures.

Necessity is the mother of invention. When applied to our case, we
are unlikely to develop a preparedness against significant oil supply disruptions until such time as the event demands it. Of course, it's too late at
this point. If history foretells the future, we're likely to forget any lessons
learned from the disruption shortly after the crisis abates. America has
already forgotten that Hirohito attacked Pearl Harbor because Japan's oil
supplies were effectively disrupted.

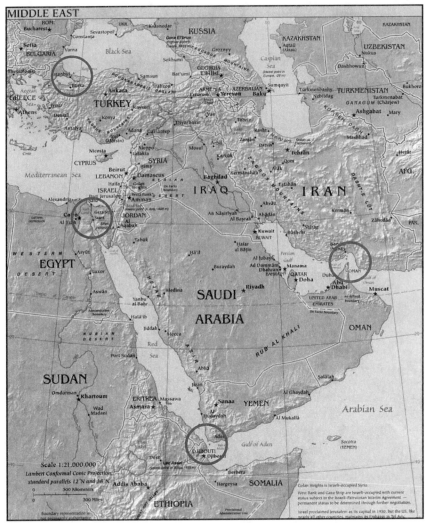

Fig. 4-4: *Asian and Middle East choke points. Source: University of Texas Library*

Choke Points

Choke points are locations in oil and gas transport routes where the flow could easily be disrupted. Daily volumes through these points are sufficiently large to cause adverse effects if the flow were curtailed. Volumes for international choke points range from 1 million bopd for lesser locations to about 14.5 million bopd through the Strait of Hormuz.

Key international choke points include the following, most of which are in the Middle East or at the Asia-Europe intersection (Fig. 4-4):

- Strait of Hormuz connecting the Persian Gulf with the Gulf of Oman.

- Suez Canal and its companion Sumed Pipeline.

- Bosporus Straits joining the Black Sea to the eastern Mediterranean.

- Malacca Straits and the adjoining Spratly Islands.

In the U. S., Alaska's Alyeska pipeline is in the same class of international choke points.

Essential supply routes do not have easily accessible alternative routes. In the case of the Suez Canal or Malacca Straits, substantial distance increases are required if alternate tanker routes are required. In addition, more tankers must be deployed to maintain existing delivery schedules.

Other choke points have no alternatives whatsoever. These include the Strait of Hormuz, Bosporus Straits and the Alyeska pipeline. Hormuz is the corridor for most Persian Gulf Oil and is the king choke point. Turkey's Bosporus Straits is the current outlet for Caspian Sea oil and much of Russia's production. Alyeska is the sole means of transporting Alaska's North Slope oil to shipping ports at Valdez.

Localized choke points exist within the boundaries of the United States and other individual countries. The oil and gas avenues from the U.S. Southwest/Gulf of Mexico supply sources to the Northeast or Midwest regions are as critical to domestic consumption as key international locations are for global supply.

ALYESKA PIPELINE

Abundant oil reserves from Alaska's North Slope are transported via the Alyeska Pipeline to the Valdez Marine Transport Terminal southeast of Anchorage. (Fig. 4-5) This construction project was a major engineering accomplishment satisfying transport requirements, safety, and environmental friendliness. As of 2002, more than 13 billion barrels of oil have

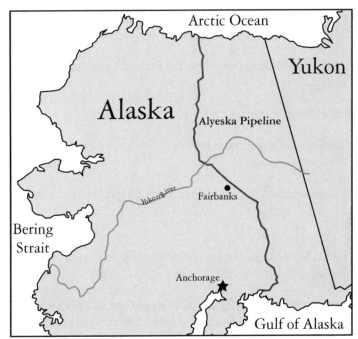

Fig. 4-5: Alyeska Pipeline runs North-South in Alaska. Source: Composite map, N. Perez

traversed the length of the pipeline. The project was, by no means, a simple job.

Alaska's North Slope is a substantial oil field by international standards and one of America's largest. Oil in place is estimated at 23 billion barrels with initial recoverable reserves of approximately 10 billion barrels. Natural gas estimates reach 25 Tcf. Average well depth is about 9,000 ft.

Environmental conditions are unfriendly. The sun does not rise for almost 60 days during winter months. Winter temperatures drop to about –60° F with wind-chill factors as low as –135° F. Summer, on the other hand, has 24 hrs of sun with temperatures that might reach only 70° F.

The Alyeska pipeline is a 48-inch outer diameter pipeline, 800 miles in length. Ownership is 375 miles federal, 321 miles state and 104 miles of private ownership. Maximum throughput exceeds 2,000,000 bopd but the current flow volume is less than 1,000,000 bopd. Further declines in North Slope production will continue pipeline rate reductions.

The pipeline has overcome many technical challenges:

- Rugged terrain with elevations from flat marsh to 5,000 ft mountain ranges

- Permafrost regions where the ground is permanently frozen year round

- Thermal induced joint expansion

- Oil temperature and viscosity control to retain fluid pump ability

Current pipeline flow rates are about 800,000 bopd. Pump stations at various locations maintain line pressure to continue oil movement. Repair facilities are located along the 800-mile length. Emergency shutdowns where the oil becomes stagnant over 21 days can allow thickening, or viscosification, such that the oil can no longer be pumped. In effect, the line capacity of 9,000,000 bbl would be frozen. This situation has never occurred, principally due to good pre-construction engineering and constant daily vigilance.

The Port of Valdez, Alyeska's endpoint, is a year round, ice-free natural fjord. Tanker approach is from the Gulf of Alaska, through Prince William Sound via the Hinchbrook Entrance with its dedicated traffic lanes to Valdez Arm and Valdez Narrows.

The port's loading capacity far exceeds pipeline capacity. It can handle tankers of the VLCC classification and almost ULCC capacity. Four berths are available with turnaround time of approximately 18 hours. The port also has a tankage holding capacity of 9.2 million barrels.

Susceptibility to attack is perceived to be lower than other international pipeline or waterway equivalents due to Alyeska's remoteness from most recognizable terrorist locations. A successful attack, however, could decommission the line and disrupt oil flow into California, a primary

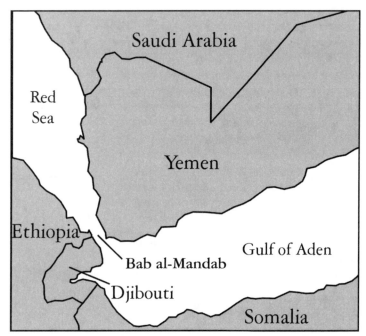

Fig. 4-6: Bab al-Mandab choke point. Source: Composite map, N. Perez

recipient of Alaska's oil supply. Alyeska has been sabotaged on one occasion to date with the saboteur being a local disgruntled source.

BAB AL-MANDAB

Western traffic from the Persian Gulf destined for the Suez/Sumed transit points must pass through the Bab al-Mandab, which separates Africa and Yemen on the Arabian Peninsula. (Fig. 4-6) It connects the Arabian Sea, Gulf of Aden, and the Red Sea.

The Greater Hanish Island, just north of the Bab al-Mandab, was the focus of a 1995 conflict between Yemen and Eritrea, Africa. Control of shipping lanes was undoubtedly part of the agenda.

Subject to flow disruption through Bab al-Mandab, some oil and gas could flow on the East-West pipeline, with its capacity of 5.0 million bopd, across Saudi Arabia to the Port of Yanbu, as well as the Abqaiq-Yanbu

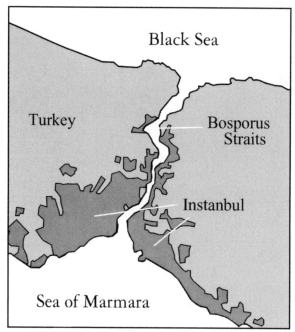

Fig. 4-7: Bosporus Straits. Source: Composite map,
N. Perez

natural gas liquids lines across Saudi to the Red Sea. However, closure
would halt all southland traffic, much of which is refined products destined for the Middle East and Africa.

BOSPORUS STRAITS

A mammoth waterway of potential terrorist targets is the Bosporus
Straits in Turkey. (Fig. 4-7) Issues include a multiplicity of targets, numerous groups with reasons for unrest, a large potential impact on the burgeoning oil industry in the Caspian Sea geo-arena and, not least on the list,
potential havoc to Istanbul and its residents. The convoluted political
structure, both from a regional and international perspective, will
undoubtedly impede positive action to mitigate the Straits as a terrorist
target.

Turkey, which straddles the Straits, is the only country spanning two
continents. Its strategic location makes it a natural energy bridge between
the Caspian Sea and the Middle East. A portion of Turkey exists on south-
eastern Europe while the major geographical area exists in Asia. At the

northeast end of the Mediterranean, Turkey is bound to the north by the Black Sea and to the west by the Aegean Sea.

The Bosporus Straits, from a geophysical view, are in a naturally formed inundated valley that follows an irregular northeast-southwest course approximately 17 miles long, with widths of 2 miles at its maximum breadth at the northern mouth reducing to 700 yards at Rumelikharsi, midway of the Straits and near the city of Istanbul. River currents of 7-8 knots flow north to south while strong subsurface counter-currents with numerous points and coves generates swirls and eddies that make navigation dangerous to the inexperienced. The complex navigational system requires course changes 12 times, with many 45° changes.

The most senior issue revolves around traffic congestion, a matter that will probably reach critical mass early in the first decade of the new millennium. In the mid-1930s, annual throughput volume was 4,500 ships whereas the volume in 2002 is 50,000 ships per year. From a practical lens, this amounts currently to about one ship each 10 minutes. Although this rate is substantive, an additional 1500 local vessels navigate the Straits daily as part of Istanbul and Turkey's domestic economy. Taken as a whole, the Straits are the busiest waterway in the world, three times more active than the Suez Canal.

Vessel size has increased since the mid–1930s when vessel length was around 40 m. Today, some vessels exceed 350 m in length, which by comparison is greater than the width of the Straits at their narrowest point.

A vessel is not 'just another ship' when its contents are considered. Issues of note are oil tankers and vessels loaded with nuclear waste, both of which were almost non-existent a half-century ago, but which are increasing at the present. According to the Turkish Maritime Pilots Association, oil tanker traffic from 1996 to 2001 is as shown in Table 4-2.

Table 4-2: Annual Tanker Traffic through Bosporus Straits.

Year	Tanker Traffic
1996	4248
1997	4303
1998	5142
1999	4452
2000	4937
2001	5500

The year 1998 includes all vessels carrying dangerous cargo. The 2000 volume represents some 60 million tons of oil, which is scheduled for increases as the Caspian Sea oil development continues.

The volume of nuclear materials transport through the Straits is increasing, alarming and causing unrest with various local groups. Recent 2001 demonstrations by Turkish environmentalists involved a flotilla of small boats surrounding nuclear waste-laden tankers. The protest came after a decision by the Russian parliament on June 6, 2001 to accept nuclear waste from other countries for reprocessing and disposal in the country's southern region of Mayak. These nuclear transport vessels travel the Straits to Russia's Black Sea ports. Activist operations related to these nuclear materials can be expected to increase.

The Bosporus accident rate is startling, with more than 350 incidents in the last 10 years. It is twice that of the Suez Canal and 30 times that of the Mississippi River. Unlike the Suez Canal, which largely flows through the desert, the Bosporus Straits flow through Istanbul, a city of 12 million inhabitants. The danger was underscored in 1994 when the Greek Cypriot tankers Nassia collided with the Shipbroker, spilling 20,000 tons of oil and killing 30 seamen. The resulting oil slick turned the waters into a raging inferno for five days, thus halting all traffic. A December 1999 incident involved the Russian tanker Volganeft 248, which split and sank in shallow waters due to winds reaching 70 mph. One of the Volganeft's four containers was damaged, allowing a 900-ton fuel spill. The list of similar accident reports seems endless.

Potential results from terrorist activity range from the mundane to surreal including:

- vessels set adrift causing blockage and potential collisions
- on-board fires
- fuel spills with sea-borne fires
- passage blockage by sinking vessels

An attack on a nuclear waste tanker in the Bosporus could endanger Istanbul's 12 million inhabitants. Permanent closure of all traffic through the Straits is not inconceivable.

Bosporus Straits History. A source of the conundrum is the political environment and its history of the passageway. The strategic importance of the Straits is such that many treaties have been put in place to guarantee vessel access. The reigning treaty is the 1936 Montreux Convention

Regarding the Regime of the Turkish Straits, which guarantees Turkey's sovereignty while also guaranteeing, "in peacetime, free and unrestricted passage to vessels of any nation carrying a cargo without delay or regulation." In 1936, supertankers didn't exist and traffic was minimal. An average of 17 ships passed daily, usually carrying grain and weighing 13 tons each as compared to the current 110-125 daily transits with vessels as large as 200 tons.

Turkey made successful efforts to regulate ship traffic in May 1994 when, citing safety and environmental concerns, it passed new transit measures. Key provisions included the following:

- Vessels longer than 150 m were advised to take Turkish pilot and guiding tugs.
- Automatic pilots for navigation were prohibited.
- Ships powered by nuclear energy, or carrying nuclear or other hazardous materials, had to report to the Turkish Environment Ministry for prior approval.
- Ship height was limited to 190 ft.
- New traffic lanes and separation schemes were implemented.
- No more than a single vessel containing hazardous materials would be allowed to pass at any given time.
- All ships must notify Turkish Authorities 24 hours in advance of intention to pass through the waterway.
- Ships longer than 200 m were allowed day passage only.
- Passage required favorable weather.

After announcing the new regulations, Turkey sought and won approval for the rules from the International Maritime Organization, an international entity linked to the United Nations.

Although the new regulations have only been loosely enforced as yet, many countries, notably Russia, have lodged serious protests. At issue is the quasi-legitimization of Turkey's new rules via the IMO as compared to the internationally recognized 1936 Treaty.

Reasoning behind Turkey's more forceful position is lucid and, to some degree, undeniable. Since the traffic was previously unregulated, most every conceivable type of vessel passed through. Lack of safety inspections or certificates of seaworthiness were common. Uninsured vessels occasionally sank without funds for salvage. Double hull vessels were rare. As an example, a Lebanese vessel in 1992, having no insurance, floundered with a cargo of 13,000 sheep and goats and is currently resting on bottom. Over

85% of vessel accidents were from non-Turkish trained or experienced pilots.

The passageway has been void of any radar or navigational control system, which has contributed to its status as 'the most dangerous waterway'. Only recently has Turkey initiated plans to install a $30 million dollar tracking system known as 'Turkish Straits Marine Traffic Data System'. It will include 15 different types of equipment such as day and night vision cameras, oceanographic and meteorological probes, satellite communications and radars. It is yet unclear if these systems will enhance traffic safety and security unless Turkey has some increased level of positive control over the Straits. Regardless of any systems that might be installed by Turkey, they have no impact on terrorists and possible attack plans.

Fig. 4-8: Oil regions surrounding the Caspian Sea. Source: Composite map, N. Perez

CASPIAN SEA

The Caspian Sea area is blossoming as a geo-petroleum power, albeit on a regional basis, since the Russian sphere of influence was exorcised with its financial collapse in 1991. Proven and probable oil and gas reserves, along with Western capitalization and technology, should develop the region into a substantive swing factor in world energy and economic balances. As can be expected, the sea of subsurface political and economic currents is gathering storm strength (Fig. 4-8).

The Caspian Sea area, about 700 miles long, is defined geopolitically as the sea itself and the contiguous state-owned land masses, including parts of Iran, Turkmenistan, Kazakhstan, Russia and Azerbaijan. Until 1991, only two powers lay claim to the region and its oil wealth, Iran and the Soviet Union, and treaties defined their boundaries. The current penta-ownership group has not resolved boundaries of the sea area, which has and will prove to be future points of contention.

The region has substantial petroleum assets, all originally developed by the Soviet Union and Iran. Proven oil reserves are estimated to be at least 30 billion barrels and total reserves are estimated from 180-240 billion barrels. Unfortunately, most of the original reserves dwindled as the Soviet Union decayed, both technically and economically. The surviving states of Azerbaijan, Kazakhstan, and Turkmenistan are rebounding at rates that suggest a strong future of economic and bargaining positions if short and long-term hurdles can be overcome.

Much like the California gold fever rampant in the mid 1800s, the Caspian Sea ignites similar hormonal responses. Proven oil reserves of 30 billion barrels are significant when compared to 22 billion for the United States and 17 billion for the North Sea. The region's possible oil reserves may easily exceed 250 billion barrels. The magnitude of this oil wealth is the primary economic motive for future development and also the source of potential conflicts.

Natural gas reserves in this area out-distance oil reserves by a large margin. Proven natural gas reserves are estimated at 170-190 Tcf while possible reserves are an additional 300 Tcf. These values rank the three former Soviet states among world leaders.

Having survived a near-death experience with the Soviet Union's 1991 collapse, the three player states, and to some degree Russia, are making a strong resurgence, both politically, economically and from a petroleum production view. The region's oil production reached 1.3 million bopd in 2001 and is expected to increase, pending resolution of transportation issues.

All does not necessarily end well as the region has an abundance of headaches facing its future. Intuitively, issues of political stability, economic viability and regional relationships must be considered. The difficulties do not end with these issues.

Much of the region's oil reserves are contained offshore. Oil drilling and production technologies, most to come from Western alliances via production-sharing agreements, should be able to prove up and produce the reserves.

The question of offshore ownership is the stumbling block. The five contiguous states have not reached an understanding or working formula as to an equitable division of sub-surface mineral rights. The potential riches in this high-stakes poker game have impaired the vision of the players. A recent confrontation involved an Iranian gunboat asserting their perceived ownership of an area being explored by a seismic exploration vessel operating for British Petroleum.

Finding markets for petroleum products and transporting the products to market customers is a long-term issue for the region. Historically, transportation in the form of pipelines has been through Russia but alternate options are necessary because the current Russian infrastructure is incapable of handling future production volumes. In addition, the existing avenues are a hindrance to future production as Russia's GasProm, its natural gas pipeline monopoly, has starved the region by refusing to pay market prices and delaying hard currency payments.

The two major pipeline proposals to handle Russian production are the Eastern and Western options, both based on future market growth. The most likely Western destination would be Europe where market size is expected to grow about 1 million bopd over the next 10-15 years. An eastward pipeline would target Asian markets where increased demand could be 10 million bopd in 10-15 years. To meet the Asian demand would require a major engineering and construction effort to build the world's longest pipeline through hostile terrain, both geographically and politically. For the present, the western pipeline proposals are being pursued.

Although numerous pipeline options have been promulgated for Caspian production, the prime candidates are as follows:

- Baku/Azerbaijan to Ceyhan/Turkey line that will provide product to an eastern Mediterranean port.

- Integration of Russia's current pipeline infrastructure to deliver oil and gas to the Black Sea port of Novorossisk, requiring tankers to transit the Black Sea and pass through the Bosporus Straits.

- Trans-Caspian gas pipeline, a/k/a Blue Stream, from Turkmenistan, under the Caspian Sea, across Azerbaijan and Georgia to Turkey. This route has several difficult technical problems including subsea pipeline construction in a corrosive hydrogen sulfide environment.

The 1000 mile Baku-Ceyhan route, part of the proposed Eurasia Corridor, is attractive, albeit the most expensive option. Western proponents favor this route as it circumvents Russia and Iran. Turkey is a major cheerleader for this option as it will be able to coffer substantial transportation tariffs, provide an independence from Russia and relieve tanker pressure on the over crowded Bosporus Straits. Oil flow through the pipeline could begin as early as 2004, barring any schedule delays.

The Ceyhan end point is a proven port as it currently handles VLCCs whereas Novorossisk (Black Sea port) is restricted to the smaller LR-2 tankers due to size restrictions when transiting the Bosporus. Ceyhan is versed in large volume traffic handling, as it is a major sea outlet for Iraqi oil exports. Also, Novorossisk is closed about 2 months each year due to bad weather; a situation that disrupts oil production practices.

Political Stability Issues. Petroleum production and transportation from the Caspian Region faces political instabilities that could disrupt oil flow virtually any time and for any duration. A disruption could further destabilize the producing region and create insurmountable, short-term difficulties for the end consumer. Sources for instability include the following:

- Turkey's failing economy requiring major IMF bail outs
- micro-regional ethnic disputes
- position jockeying for wealth and control among parties, both small and large
- Islamic-Jewish conflicts
- state-sponsored terrorist factions
- legal status of the Bosporus Straits
- special interest groups covering a broad range of topics including environment, fishing industry collapse, anti-nuclear as well as strife between Eastern, Western and Middle Eastern powers

EAST-WEST PIPELINE

Saudi Arabia has constructed and operates the East-West pipeline to the port of Yanbu. Capacity is 5.0 million bopd with current usage about 2.0 million bopd. The pipeline has the same vulnerability as any other pipeline but is seen as a lesser terrorist target due to tight security in Saudi Arabia. Also the fear factor of attacking the 800-pound gorilla can't be underestimated.

MALACCA STRAIT

The Malacca Strait, as the world's second busiest shipping lane, is the primary passage for oil tankers traveling westward from the Middle East through the Indian Ocean and then northward through the South China Sea to Asian destinations (Fig. 4-9). At 500 miles, it's the world's longest international navigational strait and the shortest route for tankers trading between the Middle East-Asian route. It courses through the territorial waterways of Indonesia, Malaysia, Thailand and Singapore. As China's oil imports from the Middle East increase annually, the Strait will grow in strategic importance between 2000 and 2020.

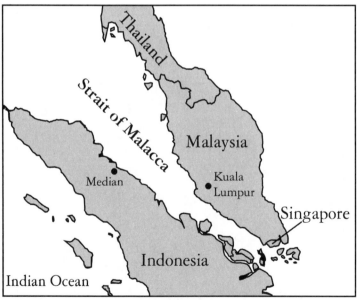

Fig. 4-9: Strait of Malacca. Source: Composite map, N. Perez

The Strait varies in width between 10-2,000 miles with water depths of 10-70 meters. It has an established working depth of 23 meters. Strong currents, shallow water depths and occasional monsoons have caused numerous wrecks to decorate the Strait's bottom.

Closure of the Strait would necessitate longer tanker routes. A VLCC requires an extra 1000 miles, or 3 days transit time through the Lambok Strait.

Although the Malacca Strait has experienced few disputed actions, the east exit into the South China Sea is less fortunate. The Spratly Islands at the east end of the Strait is a collection of mostly uninhabited islands between the coasts of Viet Nam and the Philippines and is a source of international confrontation. Principal players of China and the Philippines are eager to capture the region's unfolding oil wealth and its power position at controlling South China Sea traffic. Underlying macro-political struggles abound.

PANAMA CANAL AND PIPELINE

Panama, located in Central America, houses two potential oil targets, the Panama Canal and the Panama Pipeline. Each is vulnerable to terrorist attacks. The canal uses three sets of locks to transfer ships from sea level up 26 m to an inland lake and back to sea level prior to re-entry to the ocean (Fig. 4-10).

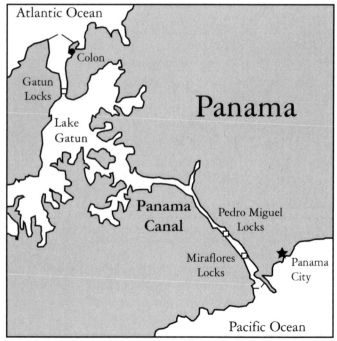

Fig. 4-10: Panama Canal. Source: Composite map, N. Perez

The Republic of Panama and the United States ratified the 1903 Panama Canal Treaty, which granted rights to build and operate a canal connecting the Pacific Ocean with the Caribbean Sea, through the Isthmus of Panama. The treaty essentially provided the U.S. with a 10-mile wide strip, over which it enjoyed full sovereign control. The Panama Canal was subsequently built and operated by the United States for over 80 years. Control was transferred to Panama in 1999 via a 1977 treaty signed by Panamanian president Omar Torrijos and U. S. president Jimmy Carter. The canal is currently owned by the Panamanian government and operated by a Hong Kong-based management group.

In 2000, petroleum and petroleum-related products were the second largest commodity, by tonnage, shipped through the canal and accounted for 14% of all shipments. More than 70% of shipments went from the Atlantic to the Pacific Ocean (Table 4-3).

Table 4-3: 1999 Panama Canal Petroleum Traffic

	Barrels Per Day				
	Crude Oil	Diesel	Gasoline	Jet Fuel	Kerosene
Originating in	2,843	9,930	39,655	2,783	600
Destined to	78,670	14,105	68,186	25,840	0
Originating in and destined to	2,210	1,596	29,020	2,761	0
Exports	633	8,334	10,635	22	600
Imports	76,460	12,509	39,167	23,079	0

If transit were disrupted, the 860,000 bopd Trans-Panama pipeline (Petroterminal de Panama, S.A.) could be re-opened to carry oil in either direction. This line is near the Costa Rican border and runs from the Port of Chiriqui Grande, Bocas del Toro on the Caribbean to the Port of Charco Azul on the Pacific Coast.

Vulnerability of the Panama Canal is borne from several areas.

- The current Panamanian president holds a slim majority.

- Frequent and often violent clashes along the Panamanian border, a spillover from the intra-Columbian political unrest, have become increasingly common in the new millennium.

- U.S.-led drug wars against Columbian citizens may illicit reprisals against the Panama Canal due to its importance for the U. S. economy.

- Panama is without a military force since the 1989 removal from office of Manuel Noriega, leaving police forces to secure the border area.

- The canal's importance as an oil transport route is diminishing. Ports on the east and west coasts of the United States receive direct oil shipments from Middle East sources that previously would have gone through the canal.

STRAIT OF HORMUZ

If ranked by daily oil transit volumes, the Strait of Hormuz tops the list without a contender in sight. The 2001 average rate was 12-14 million bopd, accounting for 40% of all world's oil trade and 80% of the oil exported from the Persian Gulf. Export destinations are eastward to Asia and westward to Western Europe and the United States.

The Strait is at the southern end of the Persian Gulf, also known as the Arabian Gulf, a 628-mile long sea. The Strait separates Iran to the east and the Arabian Peninsula to the west. Hormuz, the only sea-going exit from the Persian Gulf, is approximately 34 miles wide at its narrowest point and lies between Iran and Oman. Inbound and outbound transit lanes are 2-mile wide channels separated by a 2-mile neutral lane (Fig. 4-11).

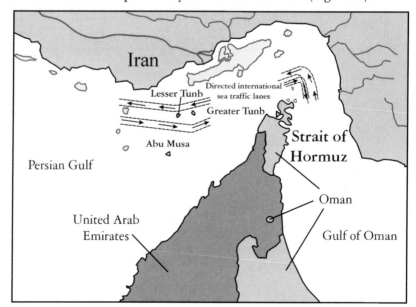

Fig. 4-11: Strait of Hormuz. Source: Composite map, N. Perez

The Strait is a contested area, principally between the entities of Iran and the United Arab Emirates (UAE) with the UAE receiving the tag-along support of the Gulf Cooperation Council (GCC). Superficially at stake is ownership of the three islands of Abu Musa, Greater Tunb Island and Lesser Tunb Island. The greater prize is control of oil transportation through the Straits. This affects Middle East economics and ultimately is a primary influencing factor on the world's industrial community.

Iran occupied the three islands in 1992 and declared them as an "inseparable part of Iran" in 1995. The GCC, a loosely bound collection of the UAE and neighboring state entities, none of which will stand alone or as a collective body in anything other than ink on a page, protested Iran's declaration of ownership and proposed that the dispute be resolved by the International Court of Justice. After a 1996 rejection of the UAE and GCC proposal, Iran strengthened its hold on the three islands by constructing a power plant on Greater Tunb, an airport on Abu Masa and initiated construction plans for a new port on Lesser Tunb. The GCC issued a statement in December, 2001 that continued its support for UAE's sovereignty over the three islands, declared Iran's claims as 'null and void', and backed all measures by the UAE to peacefully regain sovereignty on its three islands. None realistically expect the UAE to challenge Iran. In March 2000, *Jane's Defence Weekly* indicated no evidence that Iran had taken steps to convert the islands into "unsinkable aircraft carriers capable of closing the Strait during a crisis."

The future of the Strait of Hormuz is uncertain. Currently under Middle Eastern control, its importance to western society will keep the Strait in the forefront of international scrutiny.

SUEZ CANAL

The Suez Canal, the venerable statesman of engineered and constructed waterways, is a primary conduit for oil transportation of about 1 million bopd from the Middle East to Western destinations. Should the waterway be rendered non-functional, the result is severe but not fatal from an oil flow view. The alternate shipping lane would be a circuitous path around the southern coast of Africa's Cape of Good Hope and would require additional tanker fleetage to support uninterrupted supply at levels seen prior to the canal disruption.

The 100-mile waterway with a minimum width of 195 ft in some places connects the southern Mediterranean Sea with the Gulf of Suez and the Red Sea. Built in 1859-69 by the French engineer Ferdinand de

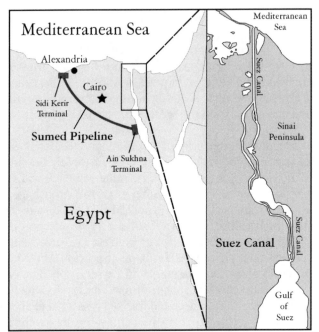

Fig. 4-12: Suez Canal and the Sumed Pipeline. Source: Composite map, N. Perez

Lesseps, the canal has the desired attribute of connecting its end points without the use of a time-consuming lock system (Fig. 4-12).

The canal was used to transport around 820,000 bopd of petroleum in 2000. Southbound trade consisted of 180,000 bopd of petroleum, around 90% of which was refined products and the rest crude oil. Northbound trade consisted of 640,000 bopd of petroleum—nearly 60% was crude. These volumes required 350 tankers.

The Suez Canal isn't immune or without scars from political and military disturbances. Its importance arising from its location will maintain the status of a prized jewel in the eyes of Arab, Jewish, and Western interests. Efforts to exercise control over the passage could originate from these sources as well as terrorist origins.

The canal hosted three wars: the 1956 Suez Crisis, the 1967 Six-Day War and the 1973 Yom Kippur War. Egypt's then-president Gamal Nasser unexpectedly nationalized the canal in June, 1956. The Suez Crisis erupted when a tripartite coalition of Great Britain, France and Israel attempted to seize the canal and return it to stockholder-countrymen. Egypt responded to the attack by sinking the 40 ships in the canal. The resulting blockage demonstrates the canal's vulnerability.

As additional testimony to the fragility of the Suez Canal, the waterway was closed to all shipping from 1967 to 1975, following the Arab-Israeli War of 1967. Cleared of mines and wreckage, it was reopened in 1975 and enlarged in 1976-1980.

SUMED PIPELINE

A companion to the Suez Canal, the Sumed pipeline transports approximately 2.2 million bopd, principally Saudi Arabian crude, northward to a loading terminal on the Mediterranean Sea. The Egyptian government has announced plans to expand pipeline capacity to 3.1 million bopd, linking the Ain Sukhna terminal on the Gulf of Suez with Sidi Kerir on the Mediterranean Sea.

As with all pipelines, the relative obscurity of the Sumed Pipeline paints it an easy target, both from air strikes and land-based attackers. Sumed is unique, and thus higher on the target selection criteria list, due to its daily volume of 2.2 million bopd soon to be 3.1 million bopd. Most of the crude oil is destined for western consumption.

MINOR TRANSPORT ROUTES

Other, lesser routes for transporting oil and gas, although non-trivial as terrorist targets are considered in the *thorns in the flesh* category. In these cases, oil disruptions would be irritating but not lethal. These locations include Iraq's Kirkuk oil region pipeline to the Ceyhan port in Turkey with a rate of 0.8 million bopd, and Syria's pipeline at 200,000 bopd.

SECTION TWO:
ACTION

FIVE:
TERRORIST WEAPONS

The principal weapons and public symbols of individual terrorists are knives, small arms, and portable explosives (Photo 5-1). The common view of terrorists is a black-hooded militant holding an AK-47 rifle and carrying grenades and automatic pistols. Although lethal on human targets, they are not as effective against larger targets or structures.

The ultimate weapons of a terrorist campaign are not guns and bullets but rather fear—the psychological condition of the non-combatants being attacked and their opinions concerning future events. The psychological aspects relate to the general mental health of the populace, or non-combatants, and the manner in which they perceive themselves and others. Although psychological matters and opinion play a role in general warfare, they are more pronounced in a terrorist campaign, principally because the populace is the terrorism target.

At the same time, terrorists have demonstrated a remarkable ability to improvise weapons as well as use conventional warring tools in their quest for disruption. Each page in this ongoing saga seems to tell of an existing weapon used in a

Photo 5-1: Common terrorist weapons.

new manner. Hijacking and suicide bombing have been combined to create the suicide hijacker. Explosives are placed in the heels of shoes to thwart airport screening devices. This trend of creative thinking and research is increasingly more lethal and difficult to detect.

In the case of oil terrorism, many conventional techniques are used, including:

- explosives
- bombs
- kidnapping

Other terrorist weapons that could have a tangential effect are:

- weapons of mass destruction
- nuclear
- biological and chemical
- hijacking

EXPLOSIVES

Among the available weapons array, explosives usually in the form of bombs seem to be a favorite, probably due to of the ease of access.

There might be an additional reason for the preferred use of explosives; a reason that is ephemeral and fleeting but parallels the nature of terrorism and the terrorist. Authors and researchers on the psychology of terrorism have identified anger as a driving parameter for the terrorist. Explosives may serve as a visual and audible outlet for the anger in a dramatic manner more effective than subtle weapons.

On the other hand, explosives are misrepresented when, without forethought, they are equated to evil, bad or wrongdoing, which is common in view of the current public focus on terrorism. From their original development to enhancements in current practices, explosives have positive benefits that affect our everyday life. Consider the following:

- Historically, explosives have been used in gathering seismic data to assist geophysicists in locating potential oil bearing structures.
- Perforating guns with explosive charges are used in oil wells to create paths that allow oil to flow from the underground rock to the wellbore.
- Road construction in hilly and mountainous areas would be difficult without explosives.
- Automobile engines mix and ignite an explosive fuel.
- Most mining operations would be impossible but for explosives.
- Snow-avalanche potential is mitigated.

The list of applications used in our daily lives is extensive.

As a further comment on the positive use of explosives, consider that Alfred Nobel, originator of the Nobel prizes for the sciences as well as the Nobel Peace Prize, was an early pioneer and multi-patent holder in the development of explosives. Funding for the Nobel prizes, in part, was derived from profits relating to Nobel's work with explosives.

Since explosives are anticipated to be the weapon of choice for oil industry targets, we need to understand the nature of explosives, how they have been packaged, how they are expected to be packaged, and the telltale warning signs. The subject is expansive and a discipline unto itself.

The definition of an explosive is a single or mixture of substances that by their own energy are capable of producing an explosion

An explosive, when detonated, rapidly transforms itself into a production of heat and usually gas. Explosives such as dynamite or TNT release heat and air. A sans gas explosive, cuprous acetylide, explodes by decomposing into copper, carbon, and heat but is absent of any gas, yet the violent and sudden release of heat rapidly expands air in the immediate vicinity.

Hot gases generate the devastating force. The explosion's brisance is a qualitative measure of this force. Consider a hurricane or typhoon with the inherent destruction caused by winds of 80 to 120 mph. Now consider the destructive potential of an explosion where gases may reach 2000-3000° F and travel at 8,000 to 10,000 mph.

> AN EXPLOSION IS A LOUD NOISE AND THE SUDDEN GOING AWAY OF THINGS FROM THE PLACE WHERE THEY HAVE BEEN.
>
> —DR. T.L. DAVIS, MIT

Powerful explosions do not necessarily require large volumes of material. Have you ever known someone who had a tiny firecracker detonate in his hand while celebrating the 4th of July? The lesson is quickly learned and seldom forgotten.

Explosives fall into several categories.

- Propellants, or low explosives, contain all necessary oxygen to burn but not explode. They produce gas, which in turn, produces the explosion; typically used in firearms.

- Primary explosives, or initiators, detonate when subjected to heat or shock. Measured by the produced heat and brisance, they are used in many cases to detonate a high explosive.

- High explosives detonate under the effect of primary explosives and generally are more brisant and powerful than primary explosives.

It is easier to understand the fundamentals of brisance by examining detonation velocities. Common prima cord detonates at about 17,000 ft/sec (3.23 miles/second) to 20,300 ft/sec (3.85 miles/second). The resulting brisant gas wave moves at 3.2-3.8 miles/second, which generates the explosive's power.

COMMONLY USED EXPLOSIVES

Black powder. The forefather of explosives, black powder has a history that can be traced to the ancient Chinese. Potassium nitrate, sulfur and charcoal are mixed to form a powder that produces hot gas when ignited. If the burning powder is contained so the hot gases are trapped, internal pressure increases quickly until the container fails and the gases escape. The powder could be tightly wrapped with layers of paper to form Chinese firecrackers or it could be placed inside a sealed metal pipe, thus creating a favorite terrorist tool, the pipe bomb.

Black powder usage can be traced across the globe primarily because of its ease of mixing with a wide range of component combinations. However, its efficacy as an explosive when compared to dynamite or C4 has relegated it to virtual obscurity in today's world of high-tech compounds.

Dynamite is a commonly used terrorist explosive material with a top usage ranking roughly equivalent to plastic compositions such as C4. Dynamite was developed as a result of Alfred Nobel's efforts to produce a more stable form of the highly brisant nitroglycerin. Nobel was successfully issued a series of patents from the 1860s to 1880s for dynamite variations, many of which cover compositions still in use today.

Dynamite is a convenient tool due to its use in many industrial applications and subsequent universal availability, even in remote locations and third world countries. Usually available in stick form, its destructive ability is magnified simply by combining multiple stick units into a bundle, often connected with industrial or duct tape. Dynamite has enjoyed a reigning status as the explosive of choice, from a historical view, only to be replaced by, or at least sharing the throne with, special compositions such as C4.

Ammonium nitrate. You might think you had never heard of ammonium nitrate or what it does. In the most common forms, it fertilizes grain fields, vegetable gardens and lawns but can be formulated with other substances to be an explosive.

Commercial fertilizers can be purchased from most hardware outlets or lawn & garden centers. In a recent application, it was used in conjunction with diesel to form a 4,800 pound bomb used by Timothy McVeigh to destroy the Alfred P. Murrah Federal Building in Oklahoma City. The chemical compound, rarely considered as an explosive due to its extreme hygroscopicity, can be detonated with suitable primary explosives. It is particularly effective if sealed in containers or seeded with nitroglycerin or aromatic nitro compounds. Explosive temperature of commonly available, in solo, ammonium nitrate is about 1100 °F.

Liquid oxygen is a powerful, brisant industrial compound available in all oilfield applications. It is necessary in welding and fabrication tasks. First developed by Linde in 1895, the liquid oxygen condenses at temperatures below −183 °F. Offshore and land oil platforms and support vessels often contain substantial liquid O_2 sources which, with a minimal, non-technically developed detonator, can explode the oxygen. If coordinated with fuel tank explosions, destruction of the structure or vessel is easily accomplished.

Composition C4 is an off-white plastic (plastique) defined as a high explosive and is more powerful, from a brisant point of view, than dynamite. Truly, "a little dab will do you." It is predominately RDX with a plastic binder and remains malleable from about -70 °F to 170 °F, rendering it a tool of choice because of its powerful yet stable nature. Its high detonation velocity and formability necessary for shaped charge applications make it well suited for cutting steel, timber and breaching concrete not to mention its obvious suitability for belt applications in suicide bombings.

C4 or RDX is globally available as these materials enjoy broad and beneficial industrial applications, notwithstanding its substantial military usage. These materials are also available via the black market, or in times of supply shortages to the terrorist, they can be home manufactured with commercially available industrial chemicals and recipes.

Shaped Charges. Explosives designed to sever, or cut, thick materials such as oilfield wellheads, pipelines or platform structures are commonly used as special formed, or shaped, materials relying on the Munroe effect to escalate its severing ability. Shaped charged housings can easily be prepared by a layperson with equipment purchased from any standard hardware source. The Munroe Effect, discovered in 1888 by Charles Edward Munroe, states that if explosive waves from two or more sources meet at an angle, the resultant wave, which is stronger than either individual wave, goes off in a predictable direction. By engineering the direction thick oilfield metal structures can easily be cut, even underwater.

Explosive Sources. The manufacture and sales of explosives in our modern industrialized world is a substantial enterprise. Large multi-national corporations have distribution outlets worldwide, particularly in burgeoning growth areas.

Licensing requirements for the manufacture and distribution of explosives is tightly regulated. Purchases and end-users are held to the same degree of licensing requirements. Nonetheless, illegal or black market sources are always available, and it doesn't seem likely that current buttressed security will have much effect on the illicit explosives trade.

Detonation. Most explosives are relatively benign unless detonated under special conditions. As an indication of the typical impotence, the primary disposal means for dynamite is open air burning, but the explosive can be quite destructive when used in conjunction with a detonator.

Detonation conditions vary according to the explosive material. Nitroglycerin becomes unstable with bouncing or jarring and may detonate under normal handling conditions. Dynamite, TNT, or variations of plastique require small detonations, usually with an explosive material that can be activated under less strenuous conditions than required for the primary explosive substance.

Historically, detonators have been activated by physical means such as a fuse connected to the explosive such as prima cord. Miniaturized electronics and wireless communications offer an efficient and improved approach by negating the need for prima cord or fuses. Small electronic detonators are attached to the explosive. Remote activation by a cell phone, pager, or satellite is becoming commonplace. This method should be the terrorist's choice for strategically planned operations. He can remotely detonate one or several bombs without endangering his personnel or signaling his involvement.

BOMBS

Bombs have been used in warfare since Tsarist Russia in the 1880s. The Narodnaya Volya group is believed to have been the first group to systematically use bombs as part of warfare strategy and tactics. The group did not practice terrorism, per se, as they were selective in planning their attacks and attempted to avoid inflicting harm on the non-combatants.

Since the Russian advent of bomb warfare, the practice has grown and matured to our current level of sophistication where high altitude laser guided bombs are capable of hitting precise targets. Moving from precision to size, the Daisy Cutter bomb with its 15,000-pound explosive capacity was used effectively to destroy caves buried in Afghanistan.

The delivery vehicle is as crucial as the bomb itself. Current events in the Middle East raise public awareness of cars and humans used in the delivery of explosives. More common delivery vehicles include pipe, letter, car, and suicide bombs.

Pipe Bombs. Pipe bombs are an excellent terrorist toy due to compactness, variable lengths, ease of home manufacture, and ability to be thrown substantial distances and with sufficient brisance to inflict measurable damage to human and structural targets. Components include a 1-2 inch diameter pipe, preferably metal, about 8-12 inches in length with threaded ends and female caps, of which one cap is bored to receive a fuse. Most slow burning or primary explosives are effective in pipe bombs because they don't require a detonator, as would be the case if high explosives were used. Materials for pipe bomb construction are available in most hardware stores.

Photo 5-2 shows a pipe bomb, remotely activated explosives, and a gasoline firebomb. Each is home made in less than one hour and costs under $25.00 each (cell phone not included!).

Photo 5-2: Pipe bombs, remote activated explosives, and gas bombs are easily fabricated. Source: Neal Adams

Attacks against large structures such as oilfield wellheads, tank batteries, separator facilities, and refineries may require pipe bombs larger than those used against human targets. Diameters of 2-3 inches with lengths of 12-18 inches will sever most wellheads including heavy, multi-casing heads rated at 15,000 – 20,000 psi.

Letter Bombs. The oldest delivery concept is the letter bomb where explosives are prepared to appear as a letter or package and sent through a postal delivery system. In the 18th century, Johann Most originated the concept of letter bombs while working for a munitions manufacturing company. He was believed to be an advocate of terror but not a practitioner. Interestingly, he also founded the precursor to the current Anarchy Cookbook, the recognized bible of recipes and other nefarious hobbies for anarchists and extremists groups.

Postal authorities have developed hints and guidelines to assist in bomb detection. (Fig. 5-1) Many indicators of a potential letter bomb are easy to detect such as protruding wires, strange odors or oil stains. Other indicators include writing on the package that may have misspellings or badly written addresses, but these also describe a substantial portion of legitimate packages and letters.

The University of Adelaide, Australia, has developed some simple tests to assist in bomb threat analysis (Table 5-1).

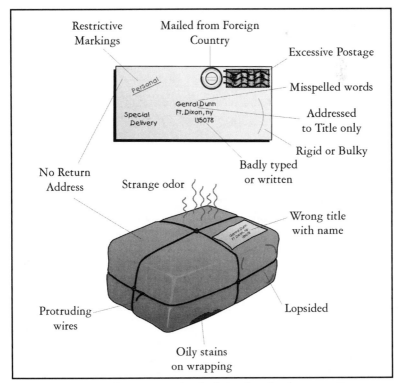

Fig. 5-1: U.S. Postal Service guides for letter bomb protection. Source: United States Postal Service

Table 5-1: Bomb Threat Analysis

Balance	Device components may shift and tend to 'unbalance' an item of mail leaving it feeling 'unusual' as compared to other similar items of mail.
Sweating	Some chemicals used in explosives may 'sweat' and result in 'greasy' marks on wrappings.
Odors	Chemicals may have unusual odors, quickly sensed by the nose. For example, notice the smell of fertilizer next time you do gardening, as it makes an effective bomb. The Oklahoma City bomb was made with fertilizer.
Feel	Letters have a normal 'feel'. Those that contain devices may simply not 'feel' right, or they may be stiff. This can indicate the presence of plastic or metallic components as opposed to the normal paper stuffing.
Packaging	Be cautious of envelopes or packages found within other packages, as it may be an attempt to mask or hide the actual explosive device.
Addressing	Be aware of items marked 'to be opened only by...'. Also, be cautious of a strange place of origin, script, disguised or unusual writing or type, obvious misspellings or word alterations in the address field or the lack of a return address.

Detection and threat analysis is more difficult than it might seem. A skilled practitioner prepares the weapon to resemble an average piece of mail.

Malcolm Forbes has offered some good business advice that also has application when dealing with opening your mail:

> *When in doubt.........don't!*

Although doubtful that Mr. Forbes had letter bombs in mind, his advice provides a good guideline when faced with this situation. If any suspicious article is observed, immediately leave the area and notify authorities. Rely on a properly trained first responder and leave the heroics for another day.

Car Bombs. Any transportation vehicle can be used to move a bomb to its target area. This includes cars, light trucks, SUVs, jeeps, and rental mid-size trucks such as the Ryder vehicle used in the Oklahoma City attack or by Arab terrorists in the 1993 World Trade Center bombing.

Cars and trucks offer advantages over other types of bombs. The vehicle has a large payload, which can be hidden in the trunk or boot. Its mobility is greater when moving into and exiting a site.

Suicide Bombs. Commonly viewed as an individual with explosives strapped around his/her waist, this picture of a suicide bomber must be broadened to include scenarios such as 9/11. As of the middle of 2001, over 300 suicide attacks had been reported in 14 countries by 17 organizations.

Although suicide attack techniques date back to at least the 11th century assassins, the current form of suicide attacks started 1983 in Lebanon. A relatively unknown group at the time, Hizballah coordinated the initial bomb attack against the American Embassy in Beirut followed by successive attacks on the U.S. Marine headquarters and the French Multinational Force in October, 1983. The last two were executed simultaneously, resulting in 300 casualties. This made a lasting impression on world public opinion and terrorism organizations.

Suicide bombings have several tactical advantages over other terrorist techniques:

- simple and low cost operation
- requires no escape routes or complicated rescue operations
- high probability of mass casualties and extreme damage
- in real time, a suicide bomber chooses the exact time, location, and circumstances of the attack
- no fear of cell compromise from a captured, interrogated bomber
- stunning public and media impact from a sense of helplessness

Another advantage of suicide bombs as a terrorist tool is low cost. Evidence is provided by a terrorist invoice from Al-AQSA Martyrs Brigade to Fouad Shoubaki of the Palestinian Authority's financial administration which include an entry entitled "cost for various electrical components and chemical supplies (for the production of charges and bombs)," citing the cost of a commercially prepared bomb as about 700 shekels or US $150.00.

Explosives used by the shihad bomber have run a spectrum of black powder to C4 and crude-to-sophisticated detonation electronics. Initially, black powder was the common suicide explosive as it could be easily prepared in back rooms with chemicals from everyday home-used products. Black powder's propensity to fizzle rather than explode paved the path for

TATP, another homemade brew. TATP is prepared from nail polish remover, hair bleaching products, and acid, and is claimed to have been used by Richard Reid, the shoe bomber, who attempted to blow up an American Airlines flight in December, 2001. The succession lead to high brisance materials such as C4 and RDX, both of which are stable products.

From an oil industry view, suicide attacks seem senseless against targets of remote wellheads, separation facilities, pipelines, and compressor/pumping stations. Likely targets are important oil facilities or choke points where collateral personnel are present:

- large refineries
- offshore platforms
- land-based loading terminals
- electronic control centers for pipelines, shipping, etc.
- tanker traffic in choke points such as the Bosporus Straits, Suez Canal, or the Straits of Hormuz

In most cases, non-suicide attacks offer equal or better advantages to the terrorist groups. The bomber can plan the attack for a time of his choosing when detection is less likely.

KIDNAPPING

Kidnappings have evolved to an everyday occurrence because it is a lucrative business, particularly in some third world countries. This practice is likely to continue, particularly in the oil industry.

> VIRTUALLY EVERYDAY...
> AN INNOCENT PERSON
> IS KIDNAPPED SOME-
> WHERE IN THE WORLD.
>
> —TERRY WAITE
> HOSTAGE NEGOTIATOR,
> FORMER HOSTAGE

Criminal justice experts, criminologists, and social scientists have identified three types of kidnappers. They include (1) the political kidnapper or terrorist, (2) mentally disturbed or mentally ill, and (3) the criminal kidnapper. Each has differences in their reasons for kidnapping, but the common thread is that terror is caused in all cases.

Common sense is the most effective means to avert becoming a kidnap victim. If traveling to a foreign country, confer with several travel authorities such as the U.S. Embassy and the Chamber of Commerce in that country, your travel agent and the State Department about the relative safety of your destination. The Internet is a good information source. Choose a hotel in a safe area of the city or country. Large hotels are often safer. Spend more for a good hotel instead of pinching pennies and choosing a shambles in a poor area. When walking around the hotel and certainly when venturing outside, don't advertise by wearing your new Rolex. Leave those big diamond rings at home or locked in the hotel safe. A thief can quickly chop off a hand to steal an expensive watch.

If employment makes you a kidnap target, your company should consider retaining experts in Executive Personal Protection, or bodyguards. A good personal protection expert is likely to avoid placing you in a dangerous situation. They typically will spend time planning and researching to avoid situations where force might be required. Unlike in the movies, karate stars seldom make good bodyguards.

HIJACKING

Fortunately for the oil industry, a silver lining may exist to the aircraft hijacking cloud. Attempts to conceive an oil target worthy of terrorist hijacking efforts fails to produce candidates. Logic suggests that hijackings are directed at substantive human casualties and associated publicity.

However, during development of this section, my editor asked the question, "Is the possibility that a hijacking would be used to blow up a refinery or other major facility slim to none?"

My answer: " It is on the same scale as a possible attack on the WTC towers."

NUCLEAR WEAPONS AND DIRTY BOMBS

Nuclear weapons as a primary attack instrument against an oil target do not appear to warrant serious consideration, at least for the foreseeable future. Public opinion, strongly influenced by mass media, currently equates human casualties to nuclear events, and nuclear weapons appear at first glance to be a human targeted technique.

It is probable that terrorists, or at least terrorist states, already possess these weapons. Few can argue the India, Pakistan, North Korea, and

China possess nuclear weapons and also have government staffers sympathetic and supportive of terrorist factions.

Even if a limited nuclear war is targeted at humans, of concern here are the collateral effects on the oil industry. Consider the Indian-Pakistani confrontation in 2002 where a potential nuclear war was the big issue. Although possessing nuclear weapons, the respective delivery capability of these countries has not been addressed. This is a case where rocket science is required. It is believed that Indian and/or Pakistan rocketry may be unreliable and that nuclear delivery could be off target. Oil sites such as Iran in the west or India's Bombay Field or east coast could be impacted. It is reasonable to conclude a nuclear attack, even limited in scope, could adversely affect oil producing regions or countries.

A less obvious danger exists from nuclear weapons, i.e., the length and effect of the aftermath of the attack. Most informed sources believe the nuclear shadow will be uninhabitable for generations. The same applies to the usefulness of the applicable landmasses. To illustrate, a nuclear detonation in the Persian Gulf, even on a limited and unintentional basis, renders this world oil source radioactive and unusable, without a suitable replacement source. Although it might seem unlikely that current Arab terrorists will initiate this type of devastation, only a small step of the imagination is required to visualize numerous anti-Arab factions capable of executing the operation. Regardless of the terrorist source, the ripple effect would shift world events.

Another problematic scenario arises from the nuclear race—accidental release of radiation. Countries involved in the current nuclear race include Pakistan, India, Iran, Iraq, and Syria; none of these countries has demonstrated a history of safe nuclear operations. In most cases, the nuclear capability is taken from other countries including Russia, China, and North Korea. The acquiring country lacks familiarity with the original development of any product. Accidental radiation releases cannot be discounted and should be expected.

Consider a Chernobyl-like event in Iran or Iraq. Each country produces oil quantities capable of tipping a global supply-demand balance if disrupted. Further, consider a radiation release in Iran that affects shipping through the Strait of Hormuz, the only shipping door for Persian Gulf oil passage to world users. Although this point is made using nuclear radiation as the WMD, a similar point could be made from biological or chemical weapons.

DIRTY BOMBS

Recent history has put a new face on an old weapon, that new face being the dirty weapon or dirty bomb. Radioactive materials are combined with an explosive dispersant. As yet, the technique has not been used.

The ability to contaminate large cities is within the weapon's scope. David Kyd, spokesman of the International Atomic Energy Agency based in Vienna, was questioned

> **"U.S. SAYS IT HALTED AL-QUAEDA PLOT TO USE 'RADIOACTIVE BOMB'"**
>
> **TRACES OF TERROR: THE INVESTIGATION**
> **NATIONAL DESK, JUNE 11, 2002**

as to the practicality of making a dirty bomb of lethal proportions. "It is entirely imaginable," was his summation in comments made after the IAEA adopted a resolution at its annual general assembly that reinforces the necessary measures to protect nuclear plants. The September 21, 2001, resolution particularly earmarked the necessity of "...physical protection in preventing the unauthorized removal of nuclear material and the sabotage of nuclear facilities and nuclear materials by individuals or groups..."

Explosives and nuclear experts take different views on the bomb's long-term effect. The issue of radioactive decontamination, or lack thereof, is the crux of the debate. A 'no contest' argument can justifiably be proffered that decontamination ability, technology, and equipment is an off-the-shelf service. An equally valid position is that decontamination has only been exercised on a micro level such as accidental releases in laboratories and singular events such as the 1979 Three Mile Island incident, but it has never been tested on a macro, citywide level.

A question arises as to the source of radioactive materials for a dirty bomb. Radioactive materials capable of a controlled nuclear reaction are closely guarded at most global facilities. On the other hand, spent nuclear fuel has no commercial value except perhaps to a terrorist. Disposition tends to have less stringent materials tracing and handoff requirements than initial acquisition.

Although western countries typically practice stringent disposition guidelines, other worldwide sites are not as strict. Rumors abound frequently about Russia's escaping nuclear scientists and materials. If weapons-grade radioactive sources can change hands covertly, it seems likely that an undesirable spent material could disappear more easily.

It should also be noted that the Russian Duma, on June 6, 2001, voted to accept nuclear waste from other countries for reprocessing and disposal in the country's southern region of Mayak. The Parliament's incentive for the move is not clear, but the potential ramifications, particularly for dirty bomb users, are alarming.

WEAPONS OF MASS DESTRUCTION

The term *Weapon of Mass Destruction* (WMD) describes any weapon with the ability to achieve a large number of casualties. This group usually is considered to be chemical, biological, and radiological/nuclear events and excludes high explosive munitions packages, although the boundary line between these groups is becoming more obscure.

An Israeli research project on non-conventional terrorism recorded 292 incidents of biological, chemical, and radiological/nuclear terrorism that occurred between 1970–1998. The rate increased annually. Acceleration was due in part to recent publicity associated with these events and the on-going arms proliferation race.

The public view of WMD is changing from that of a catastrophe to a commodity. The perception of a Hiroshima-type event that causes shifts in the course of humanity has altered. Too frequently, the weapons are being discussed as a common occurrence. A casual attitude in this matter may prove regrettable.

Chemical, biological and radiological material, as well as industrial agents, can be dispersed in the air we breathe, the water we drink, or on physical contact surfaces. Dispersion methods may be as simple as opening or placing a container in a heavily used area, using conventional garden/commercial spray devices, or as elaborate as detonating an improvised explosive device. Some current long-range rocketry is capable of carrying bio or chemical-laden canisters distances exceeding 1500 miles.

Each group is characterized differently according to symptoms and timing.

- Chemical incidents are characterized by rapid onset of medical symptoms (minutes to hours) and easily observed signatures (colored residue, dead foliage, pungent odor and dead insect or animal life).

- Biological events have symptom onset requiring days to weeks and there typically will be no characteristic signatures. Because of the delayed onset, the area affected may be greater than chemical incidents due to migration of infected individuals.

- For small exposures to radiological/nuclear events, symptom onset requires days to weeks, with no characteristic signature and unrecognizable by the senses. They are colorless and odorless.

Events occur worldwide for numerous causes. Some include:

- Tylenol tampering incident in the U.S. during the 1980s

- Rajneshee cult incident in Oregon in 1984 involving 751 victims of food poisoning

- Aum Shinrikyo (AUM) sarin attack on a Tokyo underground in 1995, and other AUM attacks with botulinum strain

- Anthrax attacks spread over a dozen countries in 2001

Countries or groups interested in obtaining WMDs typically are void of the required indigenous talent and equipment and thus are forced to look outside their borders. Historically, the principle suppliers have been Russia, China, and North Korea with an occasional supply link to western sources. Current international political pressure against WMD proliferation has slowed the process but is far short of a complete cessation. Recently, suppliers have been urging self-sufficiency by the end users as a means to curtail any required on-going involvement.

Countries acquiring WMD materials include Iran, Iraq, North Korea, Libya, Syria, Sudan, India, Pakistan, and Egypt. In most cases, requisite materials, technology, and expert personnel are brought in to set up and run the appropriate facilities.

Efforts to police proliferation have achieved limited success. With respect to the suppliers, most are in a weak financial position, and the hard currency generated from the sale is important to the survival of their economies. Further, most items on a WMD shopping list are dual-application technologies, rendering it difficult to determine sales destined solely for military applications.

Acquisition by Known Terrorists

The U.S. has become painfully aware that terrorists, particularly international terrorists, are pursuing and have acquired WMDs. Iraq's Saddam Hussein has publicly stated his intent for a "Nuclear Mujhadin" to defeat the enemy. The status of his efforts is left to speculation.

Corriere della Sera, the Italian newspaper, reported in May, 1998 that Al-Qaeda had acquired three chemical and biological agent production laboratories from the former Yugoslavia. The package was complete with radioactive materials and pesticides from Ukraine along with experts in chemistry and biology. The factories were relocated to Afghanistan and Bosnia.

Al-Qaeda, through Osama bin Ladin, has acknowledged their desire for WMDs. Bin Ladin was forthright about his intentions to acquire WMDs and "spare no expense" when he was interviewed by *Time Magazine* in January, 1999:

> *Acquiring weapons for the defense of Muslims is a religious duty. If I have indeed acquired these weapons, then I thank God for enabling me to do so. And if I seek to acquire these weapons, I am carrying out a duty. It would be a sin for Muslims not to try to possess the weapons that would prevent the infidels from inflicting harm on Muslims.*

His plans leave little room for interpretation.

Saudi Arabia has received much of the focus of bin Ladin's comments. If the terrorist leader chooses to target Saudi Arabia with nuclear weapons, the consequences are unthinkable. The same issue applies if Iraq's Hussein targets Iran, Kuwait, or other of his Middle Eastern neighbors.

Biological Weapons

An anthrax attack on an oil operator was recently uncovered and other bio-threats are anticipated. The scope ranges from aerosol dissemination of anthrax spores to food contamination. An additional threat in the future is genetically engineered, drug resistant pathogens.

Sources of bio-organisms vary but, according to the Working Group on Civilian Biodefense, anthrax, bacillus anthracis, is one of the most serious forms capable of causing disease and death sufficient to cripple a city or region. In addition to anthrax, numerous other organisms pose risks to public health and national security. The Center for Disease Control and Prevention (CDC) has ranked the organisms into 3 groups, A-C, where A has the highest risk and C the lowest risk. The high risk group, A, receives the top ranking because:

- can be easily disseminated or transmitted person-to-person
- cause high mortality, with potential for major public health impact
- might cause public panic and social disruption
- require special action for public health preparedness

The group of agents includes:

- variola major (smallpox)
- Bacillus anthracis (anthrax)
- Yersinia pestis (plague)
- Clostridium botulinum toxin (botulism)
- Francisella tularensis (tularaemina)
- filoviruses
- arenaviruses

Group B is characterized by:

- moderately easy to disseminate
- causes moderate morbidity and low mortality
- requires specific enhancements of CDC's diagnostics capacity and enhanced disease surveillance

The group includes:

- Coxiella burnetti (Q fever)
- Brucella species (brucellosis)
- Burkholderia mallei (glanders)
- alphaviruses
- ricin toxin from Ricinus communis
- epsilon toxin of Clostridium perfringens
- Staphylococcus enterotoxin B
- Salmonella specie
- Shigella dysenteria
- Escherichia coli O157:H7
- Vibrio cholerae
- Cryptosproidium parvum

The lowest priority group, C, includes emerging pathogens that presently are low risk but could be engineered for mass dissemination in the future due to:

- availability
- ease of production and dissemination
- potential for high morbidity, mortality, and major health impact

These include:

- Nipah virus
- hantaviruses
- tickborne hemorrhagic fever viruses
- tickborne encephalitis viruses
- yellow fever
- multidrug-resistant tuberculosis

Global conventions have attempted to halt or retard bio-proliferation. The Biological Weapons and Toxins Convention was an effort to define bio warfare limitations, with a focus on biological attacks. Its intent was to prohibit offensive biological weapons research or production and was signed by most global participants. Iraq and the Soviet Union, both convention signatories, have subsequently acknowledged having offensive biowarfare programs; a number of other countries are believed to have such programs, as have some autonomous terrorist groups.

Bio-Attack Sources

Foreign and domestic sources are actively pursuing, and have obtained, bio-attack materials. As a current example, bin Ladin and Al-Qaeda have vigorously pursued the acquisition of biological agents for terrorism purposes. The British expert, Simon Reeve, claims that Al-Qaeda agents in Albania have obtained vials of anthrax and botulinum toxin from sources in the Czech Republic. During the trial of an Egyptian militant, allegations were made that Al-Qaeda had acquired the deadly Ebola virus in addition to anthrax.

Authorities are investigating the development status of genetically engineered, drug resistant pathogens. Russia is known to have developed a virus strain not susceptible to currently available antibiotics. Unless the U.S. is successful in achieving greater bio-cooperation with Russia, it seems almost certain that these engineered pathogens will be commercially distributed to third world countries, similar to other biological and chemical agents.

Bio-attacks instigated by an Arab country on a neighboring country have a significant oil impact. The effect is similar, but on a lesser scale, to the consequences of a nuclear attack or significant radiation leak.

Chemical Weapons

Chemical agents as warfare agents range from chemicals commonly used in the oil industry to toxic materials and designer toxins. The CDC Strategic Planning Workshop of April 2000 has established priorities for ranking chemical agents as war tools:

- already known to be used as weaponry
- availability to potential terrorists
- likely to cause major morbidity or mortality
- potential for causing public panic and social disruption
- agents to require special action for public health preparedness

Also, the CDC has identified various chemical agent categories:

- nerve agents
- blood agents
- blister agents
- heavy metals

- volatile toxins
- pulmonary agents
- incapacitating agents
- pesticides
- dioxins, furans, and polychlorinated biphenyls (PCBs)
- explosive nitro compounds
- flammable industrial gases and liquids
- poison industrial gases, solids, and liquids
- corrosive acids and bases

Agent applications are comparable to biological terrorist weapons with the primary exception that symptom onset is quick rather than delayed.

An attack in a factory producing dangerous chemicals could result in serious consequences. Sufficient explosives detonated during windy, turbulent weather conditions could disperse airborne particles over a large geographical area. Oil refineries and chemical plants fall into this category.

Summary

Regardless of the choice of weapons, it will often be matched with its intended target. Knowledge of oil sites that are potential targets better defines the weapon to be used.

SIX:

OIL AS A TARGET

GENERAL SELECTION CRITERIA

Oil and gas facilities as terrorist targets cover a far-ranging spectrum from reservoirs to wellheads, pipelines, refineries, storage facilities and end market points such as common gasoline convenience stores. Some type of attacks would have only short-term damage while others could be greater.

ACCESS

Common among most potential oil targets is their relatively low level of security against an attack, i.e., they are soft targets. Even with facilities valued from several hundred million to billions of dollars, such as refineries and offshore platforms, terrorist attacks would require only a trivial effort and could cause severe damage, in some cases requiring long periods of down time, subsequent lost production, and job losses.

SECURITY LEVEL

Security for potential oil targets, particularly in areas such as the United States, United Kingdom, and Western Europe is miniscule and superficial at best. Weapons screening is non-existent at facility access points. Employee background checks against a terrorist or watch database have not been implemented. The oil industry is not unduly relaxed in this area but rather is on par with most other western industries except, perhaps, the nuclear industry.

PROCESS INTERRUPTION

Process interruption can be a consideration in evaluating oil targets. Refineries often have long and complex start-up procedures if they had been shut down using emergency conditions. Some large industrial complexes depend on a single-source pipeline to provide fuel. A targeted attack on these or similar sites can have a domino effect in interrupting normal manufacturing processes with the attendant social upheaval.

SPECIFIC TARGETS AND TACTICS

OIL AND GAS RESERVOIRS

Oil and gas reservoirs contain the hydrocarbon accumulations sought by geophysicists, geologists, and oil engineering departments. One or more wells penetrate the reservoir rock to provide a conduit for fluid extraction.

Reservoir size covers the spectrum from too small for economic production to extremely large. In special cases, a single reservoir may be sufficiently large that a country's viability as a producer-state would be crippled if the reservoir were lost or jeopardized. Examples of mega-sized, mega-impact reservoirs are found worldwide but are particularly prevalent in several Middle East states such as Kuwait's Burgan Field (oil) and Qatar's North Field (gas). If a terrorist operation were conceived and executed that rendered the reservoirs incapable of production, Kuwait and Qatar would suffer substantive economic impact with ripple effects to the production end users. The Kuwait invasion in the early 1990s did, in fact, cripple Burgan (and other Kuwaiti reservoirs). The worldwide consequences have been duly documented.

A terrorist can develop a strategy against reservoir targets by two means, (1) impact the producing conduits or wellheads as was done in Kuwait or (2) attack the reservoir directly. Although extremely difficult and considered highly improbable, a direct attack on the reservoir could cripple future production if properly planned and executed

Returning to the example of Qatar's North Field, reservoir impairment is more easily inflicted because this offshore site is serviced by two large platforms. A planned effort could cause serious damage levels ranging from significant downtime to complete destruction. Individual blowout and firefighting efforts on the large volume wells could require several years and would be a necessary precedent to refurbishing and reconstruction efforts. In addition to the obvious effect on Qatar's economy, Japan would be affected due to their financial dealings with Qatar as well as their dependence as an end user of Qatari production. Although Qatar's North Field is used as an example, similar issues exist, albeit on a lesser scale, if other large offshore platforms in the North Sea or the United States were targeted.

OIL WELLS

Underground wells, the hydrocarbon flow conduits, are hard targets on a level equal to reservoirs. From an impact view, little is served in most cases by targeting individual wellbores unless the attacker is hopeful the damage will spread to adjacent wells, as might be the case in offshore production facilities. Related damage from one land well to another isn't practical because most land wells are located at a distance from each other. Also, the wellhead is a softer target and yields the same general effect as targeting the well itself, which suggests that the wellhead is the more likely target. History shows many cases of this type of terrorism.

Wellheads are targets-of-ease, as evidenced by repeated attacks worldwide. Security levels on land wells are basically non-existent except for an occasional fence and unlocked gate. Target impact ranges from slightly greater than zero, as in the case of pumping or gas lift wells, to much greater, for high-pressure wells, particularly if they contain hydrogen sulfide, toxic components. In the case of artificial lift wells that are incapable of natural flow, i.e., pumping or gas-lift, wellhead destruction would halt oil production but would have few other consequences. The impact level of targeting high-pressure, toxic wells is a function of the well's proximity to populated areas. If the well is remote, damage falls into the costly nuisance category, whereas it can be fatal if near populated areas. Fortunately, all but a small percentage of wells are remote.

Oil and gas wells are most vulnerable above ground where the wellhead is connected to casing. The wellhead is a collection of valves that controls pressures from the well and also directs flow to separation facilities and pipelines. Diameters at the ground may be 12-36 inches and decrease to 4-8 inches at the top. Heights range from 5-8 feet.

Bomb detection guidelines for wells are based on the optimum placements for the explosives. Greater damage is inflicted if the wellhead is targeted near the ground. With sufficient explosives, it can be ruptured or severed, which allows the oil or gas to shoot uncontrolled above the ground. Hydrocarbon ignition is probable. Tell-tale bomb indicators are sand bags or other heavy objects used to wedge explosives near the wellhead to produce a greater brisant effect (Fig. 6.1). Any heavy object will serve the purpose. Typically, metal will not be used if a remote detonator is employed, which is fortunate for the bomb detection crews since most oilfield sites have an abundance of metal items on site. The Iraqi army used this type of placement on the 700-plus Kuwaiti wells destroyed during the Gulf War.

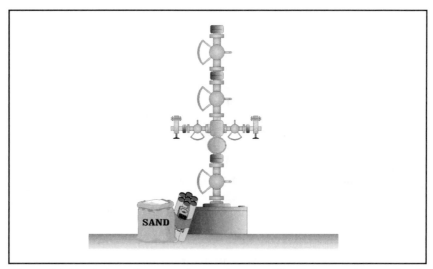

Figure 6-1: Explosives placement for maximum wellhead damage. Source: Neal Adams

Wells located in remote areas may be surrounded by vegetation or, in arid climates, covered with sand. This complicates bomb inspection efforts (Photo 6.1).

Photo 6-1: *Growth around isolated wellhead and oil facilities increase difficulty of bomb detection. Source: Neal Adams*

Any oilfield worker can detect suspicious devices that might be bombs. Be aware of anyone exhibiting unusual behavior. This might be individuals working around wellheads or other potential targets who do not look familiar, who act as if they are uncomfortable, or who are in a hurry. Most personnel unfamiliar with oilfield equipment are tentative when in the immediate area.

If an unusual object is discovered, personnel should immediately leave the area and verify that all other workers are clear of the site. Notify authorities such as the sheriff's office, police, fire department, or emergency rescue services and request a first responder team. When the authorities arrive on location, let the experts handle the situation.

Photo 6-2: Pipelines are high visibility targets. Source: Neal Adams

PIPELINES

As of 1997, the U.S. natural gas pipeline grid for the lower 48 states was operated by 85 distinct pipeline companies with 200,000 miles of pipelines, thousands of compressors, and numerous storage facilities. Of the 48 states, 27 are nearly 100% energy dependent on this gas delivery system.

Pipelines define the lower end of soft targets. Routing through long distances of remote terrain prohibit even modest security. Although the pipelines are usually buried over most of the route, they are exposed at river crossings and other junctures. In all cases, regulations mandate pipeline warning signs at all crossings, even though the pipeline may not be exposed at the surface (Photo 6.2). Pumping and compressor stations along the route are as vulnerable as the pipeline itself.

Trunk lines are large diameter systems that accommodate huge daily flow rates necessary to satisfy the end user market (Photo 6-3). If pipeline construction economics are considered, an important design factor is line sizing. Increasing line size, say from 12 to 24 inches in diameter will double the construction cost while providing a six-fold increase in pipeline capacity. The large increase results from gas dynamics and PVT (pressure-volume-temperature) influences. Likewise, increasing the design size from 24 to 48 inches gives an additional six-fold increase.

Although a seemingly docile issue when initially considering line size increases to meet production capacity requirements, the soft underbelly

Photo 6-3: Major pipelines are unsecured at river and highway crossings.
Source: Neal Adams

becomes apparent if terrorist attacks are factored into the equation. Large diameter pipelines, by design, reduce the number of required lines. In turn, this increases the impact if one or more lines are damaged. A straightforward concept, the sensitivity increases when considering that pipeline corridors to the U.S. Northeast or Midwest are relatively narrow at key junctures, increasing pipeline density and the ease of multiple targeting.

A pipeline's importance depends on its location in the food chain starting from the individual well to the end user. From each well, particularly natural flowing wells, a small diameter pipe is used to carry produced fluids to a central gathering system where a larger line travels to a trunk line, and so forth. The more removed from the individual well towards the collective system, the greater the potential damage impact due to increased line size and carrying capacity.

Considering the upper end of refined product pipelines heading toward regions that have large populations and industrial areas, the effect of an attack can be staggering, particularly when considering that major lines are few in number. An appropriately timed attack in the midst of severe arctic cold fronts and debilitating snowstorms would wreak physical havoc, not even considering the political, psychological, and economic impact.

Targeting a pipeline requires minimum skills. Remotely controlled explosives can be attached to any exposed line section. Many of the exposed sections are proximate to population traffic, which may give the potential terrorist second thoughts for fear of detection. Buried pipelines are protected from detonations at ground level unless large quantities of explosives are used.

When guarding against terrorist's actions, a bomb detection crew should begin with the exposed pipeline since buried lines are more difficult targets. After investigating the obvious sites, continue to areas with natural camouflage because a terrorist will likely attempt to conceal a bomb's location. Since pipelines have thick steel walls, crews should look for mid- to large-sized packages.

Regarding global pipeline systems, country-states without a strong capitalist environment or with a state owned and operated pipeline system have a notable Achilles Heel. These situations, with little or no competitive environments, are unlikely to have alternative pipeline capability and routes if a terrorist attacks a major artery. A disruption in this situation

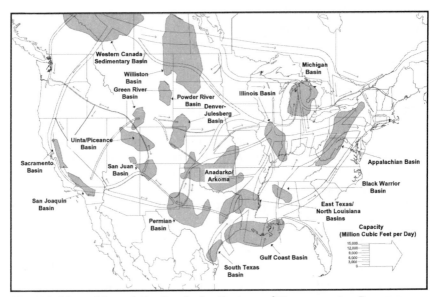

Fig. 6-3: Major Natural Gas Producing Basins and Transportation Routes to Market Areas. Source: Energy Information Administration, Petroleum Supply Annual 1997, DOE/EIA-0340(97)/1, and predecessor reports.

could have a greater effect than a similar occurrence in the U.S. where competitive pipeline systems are more prevalent.

The U.S. Energy Information Administration has data compilations and analyses useful in describing vulnerability of the industrial and domestic population to a coordinated assault on the pipeline system infrastructure. Data used herein are current to 1997 in some cases and 2000-2001 in other cases. Regardless of the date, the established trends are believed reliable and unlikely to sustain any significant modifications until 2010-2015.

The U.S. natural gas network is transnational since Canada is becoming a major supplier of gas to the U.S. and a cornerstone of America's energy supply system. Canada currently supplies 4.5 bcf (billion cubic feet per day) of natural gas, which is approximately 8.3% of the average U.S. daily consumption. The economic bonds between these North American partners are strong, which adds an overall reliability for U.S. energy supplies.

The U.S. and its Canadian gas sources have been grouped according to their major production/geological sources (Fig. 6.3). At first glance, a conclusion might be that a geographic distribution of reservoirs and basins in North America are spread throughout the U.S., which would tend to mitigate production and transportation bottlenecks. It sounds nice, if only it were true.

An insurmountable complication arises when U.S. demographic and industrial population density relative to the energy supply chain is considered. Most of the Rocky Mountains and central U.S. are sparsely populated, from both an industrial and residential point of view, whereas the Northeast and Midwest are heavy on both accounts. These latter regions are critical players from the demand side when evaluating the nation's energy requirements.

While raw data on population and industrial areas is powerful, the political and economic sensitivity of the Northeast and Midwest regions can't be overlooked. Washington, D.C., populated by not particularly energy-knowledgeable legislators, has a history of poor leadership in times of energy crises. New York, as the center of monetary power and economic issues for the U.S. and globally, would feel the business impact of energy disruptions. These areas are also centers for U.S. and global media coverage. An energy crisis would cause waves worldwide, from ripples to tsunamis.

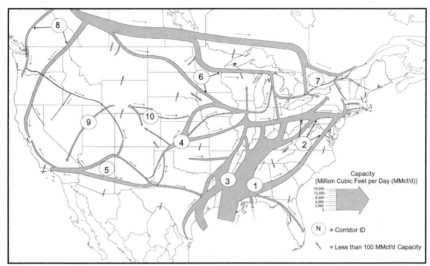

Fig. 6-4: *Major Natural Gas Transportation Corridors in the United States and Canada, 1997. Source: Energy Information Administration, EIAGIS/NG Geographic Information System, Natural Gas Pipeline State Border Capacity Database, as of December 1997.*

The discussion is further fueled when considering that the Appalachian, Michigan, and Illinois basins are unable to supply anything other than a trivial portion of natural gas requirements for these areas. The result is simple—the most densely populated and industrialized regions in the U.S. are dependent on energy sources far removed from end user sites. This situation is analogous to the overall U.S. energy scenario and its dependence on imported oil.

Most natural gas supplies serving the U.S. needs are located in the Southwest and the burgeoning offshore Gulf of Mexico (GOM) supply sources. Figure 6.4 provides a more insightful perspective of the natural gas flow corridor from source to user. Arrows have been scaled to indicate relative daily volumes. Flow paths are north and east to serve the Midwest and Northeast needs.

A focused view on Northeast requirements shows that major natural gas pipeline corridors are routed within a stone's throw of freeways in Pennsylvania, an obvious attraction to potential terrorists (Fig. 6-5). Most storage sites are located in the western areas near the Great Lakes, which requires that the stored gas reenter the pipeline system and travel eastward to serve the I-95 corridor.

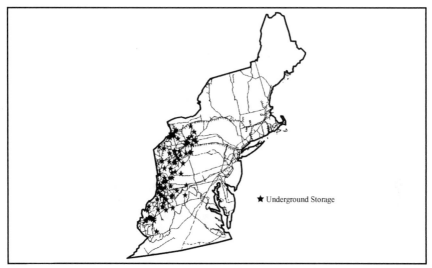

Fig. 6-5: *Major Interstate Natural Gas Pipelines Serving the Northeast Region. Source: Energy Information Administration (EIA), EIAGIS-NG Geographic Information System, as of December 1997.*

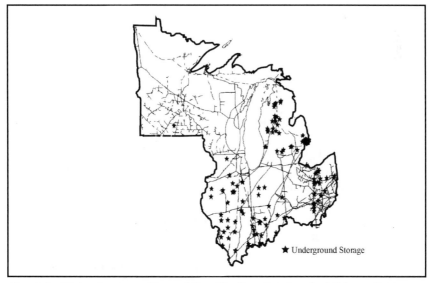

Fig. 6-6: *Major Interstate Natural Gas Pipelines Serving the Midwest Region Source: Energy Information Administration (EIA), EIAGIS-NG Geographic Information System, as of December 1997.*

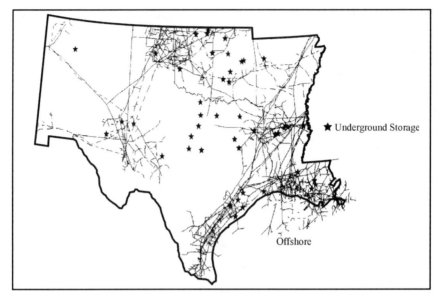

Fig. 6-7: Major Interstate Natural Gas Pipeline Exporting from the Southwest Region. Source: Energy Information Administration (EIA), EIAGIS-NG Geographic Information System, as of December 1997.

A similar situation exists with gas transportation to the Midwest Region. Flow is either from south to north bringing energy from the Southwest, or alternatively, it carries Canadian gas into the U.S. from northwest to east (Fig. 6-6). Large lines run to the Chicago area, up to central Michigan, and to central Ohio. The Midwest uses more natural gas for home heating than the Northeast.

The primary U.S. supply source for domestic oil and gas and for refined products is the Southwest and GOM (Fig. 6.7). The offshore production pipelines generally come ashore in Louisiana. Production areas are the Permian Basin in west Texas, the Texas-Oklahoma panhandle, south Texas, and south Louisiana. South Texas production passes within a few miles of the heart of Houston.

Figures 6-5 to 16-7 provide a guide to potential targets. Strategic lines are large and few in number. A terrorist would be expected to focus on these rather than smaller lines. On the other hand, smaller pipelines may be targeted because of their isolation. If a threat is received, searches along right-of-ways should be the initial priority.

The extent of damage on the pipeline grid should be discussed in consideration of each segment's line capacity level and utilization rate. These items are not constant throughout the year or, on a micro level, throughout any 24-hour period. Peak deliverability requirements are seasonal and occur during the winter, as additional natural gas is required for home heating purposes. Where average utilization might be 45-60% during summer months, it approaches 100% during winter, coincident with prolonged blasts of arctic cold waves. Assuming that an attack plan is plotted with reason, the most likely targets are big lines in the winter season.

Shortfalls in natural gas demands have an obvious effect on end users who rely on gas as a single source fuel. Homes or industries with dual fuel capability can switch to an alternative, such as liquid heating fuel, diesel, or propane. When this occurs, the deliverability burden is handed off from the natural gas pipeline grid to the alternatives. At first glance this appears simple because alternative fuel transport is usually by tractor tankers. The picture gets fuzzy due to winter transport issues such as heavy snow, ice, and arctic cold fronts. Recent history has often replayed itself on this issue.

System Capacity

The grid can deliver an average of 80 bcf under adverse winter conditions. Supply sources include gas origination or storage sites located either proximate to origination or near end user grids. As an aide-de-memoire, recall that the U.S. delivery distribution volume is not spread evenly throughout the lower 48 states but rather is disproportionately weighted to areas such as the Northeast and Midwest. Peak Northeast corridor capacity is approximately 15.9 bcf while the Midwest has 21.2 bcf capacity, or a combined 37.1 bcf to the two regions. This data indicates almost 50% of U.S. gas requirements are transported to a geographically small area.

Interruptible Fuel

Some U.S. end users have installed equipment to provide a dual fuel system, i.e., natural gas and heating oil. With this flexibility, an interruptible supply contract can be negotiated for natural gas where gas is purchased at a lower cost than the amount charged to customers who opt for a guaranteed supply. The pipeline delivery company gains the advantage of selling additional fuel at non-peak times, albeit at a reduced cost, while maintaining the right to interrupt supply to discount users in favor of customers with guaranteed service contracts who pay a higher cost per unit of gas.

The weakness of the dual fuel system is the potential increase in demand for alternative fuels, predominantly home heating oil, if the interruptible supply is curtailed. Senator Joseph Leiberman noted the issue in a February 4, 2000, letter to Bill Richardson, then Secretary of the Department of Energy:

> *This type of interruptible contract may have the unintended consequence of contributing to heating oil spikes and supply shortages. It has and may continue to account for unanticipated demand for home heating oil; these additional demands have the capacity to cripple the market in times of stress.*

STORAGE

Natural gas storage is a vital adjunct to the pipeline grid. Gas (and oil) production at the wellhead is relatively constant and can't be expected to accommodate daily and seasonal consumption fluctuations. Stored gas satisfies the demand deficit.

Most gas storage facilities are underground and consist of three principal types:

- depleted oil or gas reservoirs that have produced most of the original hydrocarbons in place

- salt (halite) domes that have intruded upward from deeper environments. A cavern within the massive structure is leached with fresh water, pumped, and returned via variable depth, concentric siphon strings

- Aquifers, which are reservoirs containing only water

Other types, including depleted mines, are currently being evaluated.

At the end of 1996, a total of 410 storage sites were operating with small levels of additions or expansions planned through 2004. Capacity was 3,765 bcf with a daily deliverability of 74.5 bcf at maximum capacity. The system has a 50-day supply, assuming maximum daily deliverability could be maintained until depleted. The deliverability rate can't be held constant, however, and decreases as product is pulled from the storage sites, i.e., delivery rates may be 60% of maximum when the storage sites are at 50% volume capacity.

During peak demand in winter months, these sites deliver excess requirements above the daily pipeline throughput volumes. The system works efficiently and should continue to do so—unless intentional disruptions are considered. Storage sites are located along the pipeline route but with a distance remaining between these storage points and end users. Tactical strikes on the pipeline void any temporary fuel relief from storage sites as well as arresting primary daily flow from original supply sources. Similar to the previously described concept of unused production capacity from oil exporting countries, the panacea of natural gas storage as a demand safety factor is not very reliable.

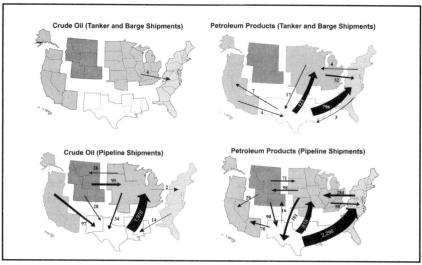

Fig. 6-8: Inter-Regional Movement of Crude Oil and Petroleum Products by water and Pipeline, 1997 (Thousand Barrels per Day. Source: Energy Information Administration, Petroleum Supply Annual, 1997, DOE/EIA-0340(97)/1

OIL PIPELINE MOVEMENT

Although not discussed in detail in this text, Figure 6-8 shows movement of crude oil and petroleum products follows the same general paths as the natural gas grid.

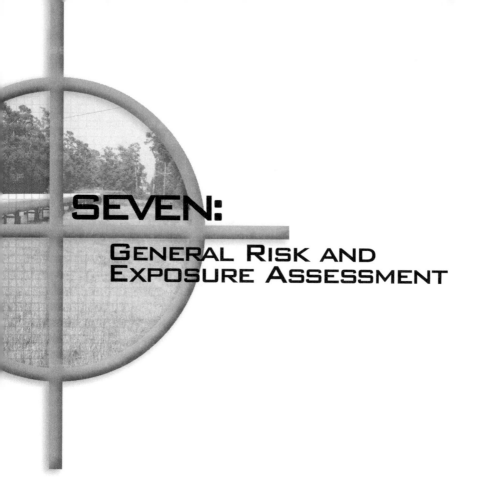

SEVEN:

GENERAL RISK AND EXPOSURE ASSESSMENT

How To Know When the Bulls-Eye Is On You!

Have you ever asked yourself, "Why should my company spend money on risk and exposure assessments when we can always call the police to take care of our problems and, besides, we spend a lot of money on insurance every year?" This is a fair question that deserves an answer.

Companies spend millions of dollars each year on insurance so why should they worry about a terrorist blowing up an oil well or damaging a refinery. The insurance covers part of the loss, but your company must pay the deductible limit, which might be $10-20 million per event. Spending a little extra effort and money on assessing and correcting risks could result in big savings.

When considering police assistance, remember that the real job is to provide protection before or during a crime. The damage will be greater if we don't prepare before the attack. Police cannot be of assistance until a crime has been committed, so protection becomes a do-it-yourself proposition.

Knowing how and when protection and security is needed requires detailed assessments to identify weaknesses. Otherwise, money might be spent on security measures at facilities where they aren't required and fail to protect others that are in the high-risk category.

RISK ASSESSMENT PROCESS

Risk evaluation is a highly refined science that can involve specialized technical expertise and regimented mathematical procedures. The reader requiring an in-depth knowledge of this science should refer to other texts.

In general, the assessment process requires the following:

- identify potential risk sites
- establish risk boundaries
- evaluate ramifications
- develop prevention plans

As an example, prior assessments for accidental oil tanker spills identified the need for, and led to, the double hull design recently introduced.

General risk types include accidents, fire and floods, storm damage and earthquakes. The recent 9/11 events have shown terrorism must be included in some assessments. It increases complexity as compared to general assessments.

Terrorism related assessments pose unique problems, particularly when applied to oil industries. The terrorist has flexibility to choose the time and place of the attack and, as such, has the ability to inflict greater damage. Consider the case of an offshore platform being assessed for storm vs. terrorist attacks. The probability of a storm causing complete platform destruction is less than a planned and properly implemented terrorist attack.

Oil has the additional risk of a fuel source inherent with the site. This can result in a fire that can burn for extended time periods at temperatures of 3000° F near the source. The extremes can range from a tanker truck filled with gasoline to high productivity oil and gas wells.

The fuel source is expected to ignite if explosives are used in an attack. This necessitates fire control services. Also, it can require blowout control specialists to stop the flow if oil or gas wells are targeted.

GUIDELINES FOR SELECTING A RISK ASSESSMENT TEAM

The oil industry is a highly technical business that involves many disciplines. In addition, oil's global nature requires the added dimension of international commerce. Performing a quality overall risk assessment of a large company's assets requires a team that can provide in-depth coverage of the required disciplines. Typical technical requirements include the following:

- geophysics, geology, and reservoir analysis
- drilling, completion, and production
- pipeline, refineries, and facilities design
- cost estimating and accounting
- security
- political and regulatory requirements
- first responders include
  - oil and gas well and facilities firefighting
  - pollution control
  - medical
  - explosive ordnance disposal

This list must be customized to accommodate an oil operator's assets and global coverage. Worldwide team experience is required for a large multinational company because operations vary significantly across national boundaries. In some cases, specialists may be required to interface with military services handling some operations, particularly in third world countries.

The team's geo-assessment and reservoir analysis requirements comes into play if terrorist attacks could substantially endanger a critical facility. An example is Qatar's North Field gas production facilities where two large platforms are used to produce the bulk of the reservoir's gas deposits. The remaining geological and reservoir assets must be quantified at the time an attack occurs. This need arises because emergency-handling procedures for first responders vary according to the oil company's future plans for the installation. If the asset is at the end of its mature life, handling procedures for asset disposal are often radically different from the reconstruction/refurbishment case.

Oil and gas wells are unique because the reservoir fuel source may be large. In some cases, it will not deplete in any reasonable amount of time, therefore the hazard resulting from the terrorist attack will not be reduced until the first responders are successful at controlling the well(s).

Effective first responses require the operator to provide expertise in drilling, completion, and production to support the first responders. As noted previously, specialist procedures are also affected by the oil company's future plans for the well.

Pollution is a high profile issue in most western environments and it can significantly escalate the consequences if an attack occurs. Third World countries tend to place less emphasis on this concern. Hence, pollution ramifications from a terrorist attack will vary with locales. Most oil companies have few pollution specialists as permanent employees and typically will rely on outside contractors to provide the bulk of their requirements. It is recommended that representatives from the outside contractors be considered for membership on the risk assessment team.

THREAT ASSESSMENT OF SITES AND RISK FACTORS

Oil and gas sites for consideration as terrorist targets vary widely. Broad categories include:

- oil and gas wells
- pipelines and pumping stations
- refineries
- tank farms
- underground storage sites
- loading terminals and ports
- tankers
- railroads
- offshore drilling and production facilities

Each is unique and will be discussed in greater detail in subsequent sections. To properly perform a risk assessment from an attack, each site requires consideration. An evaluation approach is presented with examples in the next section.

Oil and gas wells have factors influencing a terrorism assessment. They are important when designing increased security levels, first response, control operations, and reconstruction. Some include:

- fluid type, pressure, flow rates and toxic components
- adjacent enclosures
- location
- land versus offshore considerations

High-pressure wells generally produce high flow rates. If ignited, the fire and its heat may retard first response efforts. Also, blowout control operations for high-pressure wells usually require more time and specialized equipment.

Low-pressure wells often cannot flow naturally and require artificial lift production methods. The benefit relative to an attack is that, although the equipment will be damaged, it does not pose a continuing fire danger from escaping oil and/or gas.

Fluid type and toxic components have various risks. Gas fires usually burn cleaner and hotter than oil fires. Oil fires may pose pollution problems in the form of pooled oil resulting from incomplete combustion.

Some wells have hydrogen sulfide poison components, also known as *sour* gas or oil. Hydrogen sulfide is the second most toxic naturally occurring gas. This poses a risk to personnel near an attack site and requires additional time and efforts for first responders to gain control after an attack.

Evacuation of local personnel may be required. The disruption can be extensive when large numbers of people must be relocated in an area where sufficient public housing is not available.

Well enclosure structures affect the probability of an attack and the difficulty of regaining control after the attack. Most land wells are unenclosed, which eases the terrorist's job. A few wells are housed in structures resembling a fortified concrete parking lot where the wells are protected in the lower deck of the structure. These structures are used when the wells are in highly populated or industrialized areas. Although affording protection from natural catastrophes, they complicate the first responder's efforts by an order of magnitude.

Most oil and gas well locations are remote from inhabited areas. This reduces the danger from collateral damage, but it also increases the difficulty of securing the site. Since most wells do not have significant security measures, terrorists have ease of access. Its remote nature also reduces the exposure risk if an attacker wants publicity or to endanger the population.

Land and offshore wells pose control differences. First responders usually can access a land site within a reasonable time period to initiate control operations. Offshore environments require vessels such as boats, barges, and cranes that have greater mobilization times. Also, most offshore wells have greater flow capacities than land wells.

On-site production equipment is a required factor in the risk assessment. If attacked, collateral damage to both well and adjacent equipment will likely result.

The production equipment usually has reservoirs or oil tanks serving as fuel. This equipment is usually downstream of chokes that dissipate well pressure, which means that the equipment does not have thick metal walls. If the site is targeted, only a small amount of explosive is needed and it can be easily disguised or hidden.

Some wells do not have production equipment at the well site, but rather it may be centrally located when there are numerous wells in the area. An attack on a well will probably not cause damage to the production equipment or vice versa. The typical remote location of the wells and production equipment and their unmanned status allows targeting flexibility.

Pipelines and pumping stations have inherent risks because they are typically in remote locations and unsecured. Large diameter lines with high volumes pose an attractive risk as a terrorist target.

Pipelines are usually buried underground but exposed at junctures, such as river crossings, and have little security. Even the buried sections are targets because of the shallow burial depth, which are clearly marked with numerous high visibility warning signs in cleared right-of-ways. Adverse terrains such as mountains or marsh areas add complexity to the refurbishment process. Pipelines in arctic regions such as Alyeska or Siberian lines can effectively 'freeze' because the product become viscous and unpumpable during prolonged static periods. This renders frozen segments unusable.

Pumping or compressor stations offer the same destructive opportunities as targeted pipelines but with the increased terrorist benefit that they require much longer to refurbish. Many compressor and pumping stations are unmanned and poorly secured.

Refineries represent the most complicated oil installations for risk assessment of all land-based targets, and they rank high as terrorist targets. The facility's initial cost can exceed $200-300 million, which increases its attractiveness.

Refineries are typically less remote than oil and gas wells or pipelines but still can offer some degree of isolation at many installations. Conversely, some refineries are in close proximity to one another, which simplifies mass targeting. This situation is illustrated at numerous sites along the coast of the Gulf of Mexico. Most refineries have storage capacity for various types of hazardous materials. The number of daily employees, shift crews, roustabouts, and delivery personnel increase the potential for internal sabotage or selling intelligence to external terrorists.

Production capacity and the array of refined products must be considered in assessing refineries as targets. A large refinery offers a tempting target even though these facilities may have more stringent security. Feed stock or refined products can be the explosive material itself. Some refineries use or produce toxic components as part of the production process. An attack could release these components and affect both refinery employees and local inhabitants. The toxic components can easily become airborne from natural wind activity or carried aloft from thermal plumes associated with fires and explosions.

Refinery access points for feedstock and refined product transport can include road, rail and pipeline, all of which pose different security requirements and risks. Ease of transporting bombs or bomb-making materials via road or rail increases the target's risk rating.

The refinery's perimeter affects its risk. A terrorist is less likely to select a target where a harsh environment surrounds the refinery. As an example, some refineries have marshy perimeters, which are inaccessible except by airboat.

Tank farms consist of large, cylindrical enclosures holding large volumes of oil or other liquids. They may be located in oil fields, refineries, loading terminals, or even in highly populated residential areas, and, of course, the tank contents are highly flammable liquids.

Underground storage sites appear to be an obvious target. However, these sites are ranked as relatively low in importance, because damage will generally be restricted to surface equipment that accesses the underground storage system. Since oxygen is required for combustion, a surface explosion may not ignite the stored products. If combustion occurs, it will be more restricted than an explosion at an above ground storage site. Also, since most storage sites have large capacities, security and manning are often present.

Loading terminals and ports are difficult to secure and may be more critical than refineries or storage sites. Terminals and ports provide inbound and outbound transit for numerous refineries, pipelines, and tankers. Significant damage can cause bottlenecks and disruptions at facilities serviced by the terminal or port. If damaged, alternates may not be available or have insufficient excess capacity for handling the additional requirements.

Terminals have security issues similar to refineries. Many employees and transient workers may be required. Rail, road, and pipeline access must be considered. Hazardous feedstock and refined products are involved. Terminals associated with water transportation require additional security.

Tanker risk assessment varies with locale, tanker size, origin, cargo type, and loading/unloading terminals. Transit routes through areas with terrorist activity pose increased risks.

Although most hydrocarbon cargos are flammable and may fuel an explosion, jet fuel and gasoline are particularly dangerous. Spill potential is reduced with these flammable materials, however, because they contain lighter ends, or molecules, that evaporate and/or burn more quickly.

Tanker origin is a consideration in assessing shipping operations. Most large western oil companies use tanker sources that practice safety, security, and use double hull designs. Other sources may use shoddily constructed or antiquated tankers, carry inexperienced crews, lack international safety certificates, and often fail to have adequate insurance coverage. Some Liberian tankers are in this category. The situation is causing significant concerns for authorities controlling the Bosporous Straits, Suez Canal, and the Malacca Straits.

Tankers and loading/unloading terminals must be considered jointly as part of the assessment. Poorly secured terminals offer greater terrorist access to western-bound tankers. Also, risk assessment for terminals must address both tanker origin and embarkation point.

Railroads no longer play a significant role as hydrocarbon carriers. They are used to transport smaller cargo quantities to destinations not serviced by high volume carriers. When railroads are necessary, easy access and low security for railroad cars and tracks elevates their risk.

Terrorists have attacked offshore drilling and production facilities on numerous occasions, particularly in offshore African countries. The exposure is related to high installation costs, visibility, ease of access, low security, and the number of onboard workers.

Offshore oil facilities can be grouped in categories for assessing risks:

- manned or unmanned
- controlled by satellite communications if unmanned
- proximity to shore
- international location
- facility and crew size
- size, number and design of production wells and facilities
- type and volume of produced fluids
- associated transport systems for produced fluids such as pipelines, barges or variations of floating production structures

Threat sources and access methods are varied and include:

- internal employee related
- external terrorist, possibly working with employees
- boats transporting equipment or facilities personnel
- fishing boats tied-up to rigs
- local populations seeking hand-outs and traveling by small boat to the rig
- submarines
- helicopters and other aircrafts

As a general guideline, facilities located some distance from shore usually have large production capacities. They are costly—some exceeding $2 billion. An attack can cause significant damage and pollution. Fortunately, a casual terrorist usually opts for softer targets.

Small facilities located near shore are often unmanned with few security features. Many are not satellite controlled, which results in difficulty providing secure monitoring and detection systems. Also, the facilities can be accessed in small boats.

Offshore facilities must be considered in conjunction with the docks servicing the unit. Some docks and support vessels have reasonable physical security control. Control of personnel is often weak as security clearances are not required and identification documents may not be authenticated.

Most facilities have not been designed for security. They do not contain onboard security personnel, surveillance and detection equipment, or counter-attack capability. Increasing security will be time consuming and costly.

An attack threat requires pollution assessment for tankers and offshore oil platforms. If the risk is deemed to be considerable, the oil company may need to install additional security to prevent an attack or provide measures to continuously ignite any released product.

In most cases, pollution effects will be reduced if explosives are used because ignition is likely and some of the fuel will be consumed. Air pollution may occur in liquid hydrocarbon fires, but its effect is usually short lived. Oil released in a land based attack can usually be easily contained by placing earthen walls around the release site

The pollution effect can be extensive if tankers or offshore oil platforms are attacked. The sea may extinguish or mitigate the fire, during which unconsumed oil is released. Large oil platforms easily produce in excess of 200,000 bopd that could flow for an extended time period. Risk of ignition near the platform complicates the first responder's work.

Chemical or biological agents are effective in pollution containment or abatement if utilized in large quantities and applied quickly. Regulatory agencies in most western environments mandate their approval prior to application. That means, from a practical point of view, that the approval will be withheld until it's too late to use the materials effectively. The Exxon Valdez case illustrates this issue.

Another point must be made on the offshore pollution matter. Many countries throughout the world require equipment installation designed to stop uncontrolled oil and gas flow if the well is damaged. The obvious objective is to prevent pollution from a continued oil or gas flow. The equipment, known as subsurface safety valves, is effective in most cases but may fail in large disasters. An example is the 1988 Piper Alpha case in the North Sea where more than 30 wild wells flowed after an explosion destroyed the platform. All wells had been equipped with subsurface safety valves that were tested on a regular basis.

SITE SPECIFIC THREAT CRITERIA AND DEVELOPING AN ASSESSMENT PLAN

As described in previous sections, oil sites should be studied to develop a comprehensive risk assessment plan. The threat criteria described here will apply to most companies. Each may have additional considerations. A 'perfect and universal' industry assessment model doesn't exist but reasonable guidelines and checklists can be established as a starting point.

Most site models have common elements, many of which are described in previous sections. For these checklists and examples, the following issues are considered:

- impact severity
- refurbishment/replacement cost
- product type, volume and toxicity
- location
- site-related personnel
- access (road, rail, air, water)
- existing/desired security and implementation
- collateral damage potential
- damage control

Several issues affect impact severity. An attack on a loading terminal servicing many refineries, pipelines, and transport vessels has a greater impact than a small remote refinery. A large pipeline transporting heating fuel to large populated areas, particularly during the winter season, is more critical than a smaller line servicing a few wells.

Security implementation guidelines include cost and time to develop and initiate a workable security apparatus. Security against some attacks may be easier, more or less cumbersome, or more realistic than against other attacks. For example, small submarines similar to those used in drug smuggling pose a greater threat to inflict structural damage for offshore facilities than small onboard bombs.

Damage control is easier for some sites. An exploded wellhead on land can be more readily controlled and corrected by a factor of 5-10 than an equivalent capacity offshore well. Likewise, damage to a land well with heavy enclosures is more difficult to control than open wellheads.

Collateral damage to adjacent equipment and operations must be considered. A damaged component may result in subsequent explosions causing other adverse effects.

Check lists are a handy method to perform assessments. Criteria are listed, and an evaluation method is used. A common approach is to establish a numerical range for weighting the item. Examples include ranges of 1-5 or 1-10. A scale with a broader range, such as 1-10, provides the ability to give additional weight or emphasis to items with greater impact, cost, degree of security difficulty, etc. Definitions should be assigned to each scale unit so the investigator has evaluation guidelines. This avoids inconsistencies, arbitrary assessments, or human errors caused when different personnel are involved in the assessment process. Work should be assigned to team members with expertise in the given area rather than requiring one investigator to evaluate sites or operations outside his area of expertise.

Checklist items require weighting factors to properly balance the assessment. For example, replacement costs and impact severity require more weighting than fluid component toxicity. One way to balance the disparities is to use several checklists. This is illustrated in the following examples.

Descriptive comments are included for each well in Table 1-1. The checklist shown in Table 7-2 is used to assess security and risks for three different wells.

Note that general scaling ranges are offered as a guide to assessment personnel. Proper interpretation requires knowledge and experience.

Water access uses a descending scale. Easily accessible firefighting water appears on the low end of the scale. The reverse occurs if water is not available or if transportation is an issue.

Table 7-1: Well Data for Three Risk Candidates

Well #1	
Production	High-pressure oil with associated sour components. (12,200 psi)
Configuration	Deep, 2 branch multilateral complicates well control efforts if relief wells are required.
Site	The well is in a remote area. Firefighting water is available but requres a long pipeline. It currently does not have any security. Proper security requires electronic surveillance and 24/7 security teams. The wellhead is not enclosed. The well has significant on-site processing equipment.
Maturity	The well has recently been placed on production and has large proven and producible reserves.
Well#2	
	The well is artificially lifted, sweet and near the end of its productive life. It is shallow and vertical.
Well #3	
	This has medium pressures (4,500 psi) and was drilled vertically to 9,300 ft. It is a single completion with sweet gas. The wellhead is enclosed in a heavy concrete structure on a pad in a marsh site.

Tables 7-3 through 7-5 are used respectively for other oil facilities. Operators should review and refine each checklist for their particular asset configurations.

Tables 7-2 through 7-5 illustrate various techniques for evaluating security and risks. Table 7-2 provides a range of 1 to 10 without definitions for the assessor. Table 7-5 uses the same range but offers suggestions as to value assignments for common security measures. Tables 7-2 and 7-5 provide an open category for refurbishment factors not shown in the other tables. This approach was used to provide the reader with good checklists as guides—with the reservation that each oil company should review them prior to performing the assessments.

Table 7-2: Oil and Gas Wells (Land) Site Assessment

Oil and Gas Wells (Land) Site Assessment					
Assessment Criteria	Suggested Range	Assigned Value (each well)			Comments for Well #1
		1	2	3	
Type of produced fluid oil gas toxicity	 4 3 3	7	4	3	Oil 4, associated sour gas 3 creates pollution potential and requirements for poison protection.
Well pressure 0 (artificial lift/depleted) <5,000 psi 5,000-10,000 psi >10,000 psi	 0 6 8 10	10	0	6	12,200 psi
Configuration vertical directional horizontal multi-lateral	 1-3 3-5 5-7 7-10	10	1	1	Multi-lateral with two horizontal branches
Depth, measured 0-5,000 ft 5,000-10,000 10,000-a5,000 ft >15,000 ft	 1-3 3-5 5-7 7-10	10	3	5	19,050 ft (md)
Depth, vertical 0-5,000 ft 5,000-10,000 ft 10,000-15,000 ft >15,000 ft	 1-3 3-5 5-7 7-10	8	3	5	16,500 ft (tvd)
Water access	10-1	8	1	1	Available water but requires long pipeline
Location personnel safety site safety logistics	 1-10 1-10 1-10	 5 1 9	 1 1 1	 1 1 5	The well is remote which reduces control hazards and enhances safety. Jungle location requiring helicopters.
Enclosed Wellhead	1-10	1	1	9	No enclosures
SSV (Subsurface safety valve) none installed	 5 1	5	5	1	No known SSVs according to well records
Well maturity and Reserves	1-10 (depleted virgin)	10	1	5	This well is young with large reserves.
Damage containment	1-10	9	1	7	Potential for difficult control operations, relief well may be required.
Collateral damage	1-10	8	1	1	Adjacent support facilities

Table 7-2: *Oil and Gas Wells (Land) Site Assessment, cont'd*

Oil and Gas Wells (Land) Site Assessment(cont'd)					
Impact	1-10	5	1	3	Moderate overall impact if damaged.
Refurbishment factors	1-10	10	1	3	Control and replacement costs are high for high pressure wells with toxic components.
Security, current	1-10	1	1	3	Remote, no current security
Security, enhancements	1-10	8	8	8	Effective security requires monitoring equipment and guard services.
Total Site Assessment		125	35	68	

Table 7-3: *Pipeline Site Assessment*

Pipeline Site Assessment			
Assessment Criteria	**Suggested Range**	**Assigned Value**	**Comments**
Produced fluids oil gas toxic	4 3 3		
Line Diameter (inches) 0-12 12-24 24-48	5 7 10		
Location personnel road systems industrial	1-10 1-10 1-10		
Exposed surface sites/grid segment number 0-5 5-10 >10 Average exposed length (ft) 0-200 200-400 >400 Access Control none partial complete	5 7 10 5 7 10 10 5 1		
Bomb detection electronic sniffer dogs	0-yes; 5-no		
Prior Threats	(2/incident, max=10)		
Total Site Assessment			

Table 7-4: Refinery/Loading Terminal/Underground Storage Site/Tank Farm Site Assessment

Refinery/Loading Terminal/Underground Storage Site/Tank Farm Site Assessment			
Assessment Criteria	Suggested Range	Assigned Value	Comments
Products No. X toxicity	1-non-toxic 3-toxic		
Access points Road rail pipeline waterway	2/point max=10		
Access point security X no. of points none electronic measures manned manned and electronic measures	max=20		
Perimeter security none electronic measures manned manned and electronic measures	max=10 10 5 3 1		
On-site product storage	1/50,000 bbl max=10		(1/1000 bbl for refineries)
Density operations personnel equipment	max=15 5-1 5-1 5-1		
Daily staffing routine non-routine	1/10 persons max=10 2/5 persons max=10		
Location personnel road systems industrial	1-10 1-10 1-10		
Bomb detection electronic sniffer dogs	0-yes; 5-no		
Prior threats	(2/incident, max=10)		
Total Site Assessment			

Table 7-5: Offshore Drilling/Production Facilities Site Assessment

Offshore Drilling/Production Facilities Site Assessment Site Assessment			
Assessment Criteria	Suggested Range	Assigned Value	Comments
Produced fluids oil gas toxic	4 3 3		
Well pressure 0 (artificial lift/depleted) <5,000 psi 5,000-10,000 psi >10,000 psi	0 6 8 10		
Configuration vertical directional horizontal multi-lateral	1-3 3-5 5-7 7-10		
Depth, measured 0-5,000 psi 5,000-10,000 psi 10,000-15,000 psi >15,000 psi	1-3 3-5 5-7 7-10		
Depth, vertical 0-5,000 psi 5,000-10,000 psi 10,000-15,000 psi >15,000 psi	1-3 3-5 5-7 7-10		
No. of wells 0-10 10-15 >15	5 7 10		
Blast proofing wellhead deck cellar deck between wells	0-yes; 5-no		
Security none electronic measures manned manned and electronic measures	1-10 10 7 3 1		
Bomb Detection electronic sniffer dogs	0-yes; 5-no		
Daily staffing routine non-routine	1/10 persons max=10 2/5 persons max=10		

Table 7-5 Offshore Drilling/Production Facilities Site Assessment, cont'd

Offshore Drilling/Production Facilities Site Assessment-cont'd Site Assessment			
Assessment Criteria	Suggested Range	Assigned Value	Comments
Location personnel road systems industrial	1-10 1-10 1-10		
Prior threats	(2/incident, max=10)		
Platform maturity and reserves	1-10 (depleted virgin)		
Damage containment	1-10		
Collateral damage	1-10		
Impact	1-10		
Refurbishment factors	1-10		
Total Site Assessment			

Summary. This section described assessments and checklists that an oil company should use in assessing their assets. Oil industry service companies, particularly when done in cooperation with oil companies as part of an overall program, can use the same approach. As an example, Table 7-4 was designed for any multi-purpose facility.

Tables 7-2 through 7-5 do not address issues related to politics or public opinion. These factors are difficult to quantify and are often time sensitive. Cases exist where politics, and public opinion significantly out weigh other assessment criteria. Each oil and service company should account for these issues when required.

DETERMINING SITES THAT NEED PROTECTION

A primary objective of the risk assessment is to provide a yardstick to measure each oil asset. After all sites have been assessed, the next steps are to segregate similar installations into groups and then rank each installation in its respective group.

For explanation, let's consider ranking oil wells for terrorist risks. They are used here as the least complex of oil installations. Complex facilities require a more involved assessment and ranking procedure.

A ranking system should be simple. A good approach is to use categories of low, medium, and high-risk wells as a starting point. Special cases occasionally require other considerations. A broad definition of each, with examples, is provided. Note that exceptions exist for every case.

Low: This is often considered the 'throw-away' category where the asset doesn't justify the effort and costs associated with increased security and protection. Examples include pumping wells, depleted zones, excessive water cuts, or sites so remote that increased security would be difficult. Larger oil installations are seldom placed in this category.

Medium: A medium risk well typically is a good producer that has few production problems and a long life expectancy. It is located where various security levels could be easily implemented. This category can be difficult to define as some wells clearly fall into the low risk or high-risk category but others may be on the fringes between low-medium and medium-high risks.

High: A high risk well has a large asset value or impact severity deserving extra protection. Examples include high flow rate wells with large proven reservoirs or toxic wells. Some wells may be in an area where adverse public opinion is the greatest risk factor. Examples are wells located in Hollywood, CA or Den Haag, The Netherlands.

Table 7-1 showed three wells with widely differing assessments. If we apply the categories above, the assessment is as follows:

Well	Category
1	high
2	low
3	medium

High-risk wells warrant security and protection. Many medium risk wells also deserve extra security. The low risk category often identifies wells that don't require any advance security measures.

Insurance limits and deductibles play a role in deciding which wells warrant extra attention. Companies with large deductible limits may choose increased security at sites determined to have high target potential. Some wells may have impact or refurbishment costs where an occurrence could exceed policy limits. In this case, the company has to pay the extra costs above the policy limit as an out-of-pocket cost. A good example is a prolific oil producer within a large metropolitan area's city limits where a high volume oil spill would be disastrous.

Making tough decisions about which wells need increased protection requires an understanding of security options. Do we need better fences around our wells? Are cameras and motion detectors warranted? Are manned sites required? Risk assessment gives companies an overview of options. Consultation with trained security personnel prior to making final decisions is recommended also.

SECURITY MEASURES

The industrial security arena offers a wide array of tools for security and protection. Some are simple, while others are sophisticated and require highly trained personnel for implementation and daily operation. In all cases, exercising common sense when evaluating and selecting security measures is the initial requirement.

Common methods for effective security management will be discussed here. These include:

- External control
    - perimeter control/fences
    - illumination
    - motion detection and alarms
    - video monitoring
    - cosmetic defense
- Internal control
    - employee management
    - IDs
    - credit checks
    - finger printing
    - checking personal references
- Security personnel,
    - police vs. private security
    - canine support

Sophisticated techniques that may be required for future applications include radar and sonar for offshore applications.

External Control

Perimeter control/fences. The best asset protection method is preventing would-be attackers from gaining access to the site. Controlling the perimeter with an effective fence prevents entry to all but the most diligent intruder. Fence design and management is not as simple as one might believe when first considering the concept.

An effective fence must meet several criteria:

- prevent intruders from going through the fence
- prohibit burrowing underground
- discouraged climbing over the top
- allow access to authorized personnel via a gate or door

Most common security fences are chain-link mesh. It discourages intruders simply because of its presence. Special equipment such as wire or chain cutters is required for penetration. Some companies offer an improved chain link design that has reinforced strands and rebar components that are more difficult to destroy. Correctional institutions for inmate control often use this design. Most oil sites require fences and the more high-risk sites might require a reinforced fence.

Solid fence designs are discouraged. The oil site may not initially be as easily accessible to the terrorist or intruder, however, it provides a measure of safety after having been penetrated. He can't be seen easily from the outside, which provides more time for implementing the attack and causing damage.

The fence bottom should be buried 18-24 inches. Ground level fences offer little protection from intruders crawling under them. Shallow fence burials can be pulled and rocked to provide enough room for entrance.

The height should be 8 ft or greater. Little protection is offered from a 6 ft fence because an intruder can easily stand on his vehicle and crawl over the top. Constantine wire is recommended for crowning the fence top. It obviously discourages an attacker from crawling over the top but it also offers protection if the attacker attempts to remove or pull the wire off the fence top.

Gates are installed to allow entry of authorized personnel. If not secured with a substantial lock and chained at all times, their effectiveness at perimeter control is nil. A sliding gate is more secure than a swinging

Photo 7-1: *Easy access to a refining and storage site through the main gate that does not completely close.*
Source: Neal Adams

Photo 7-2: *Tank farm perimeter has 2 foot gap between fence and ground.*
Source: Neal Adams

gate that has removable hinges. On all gates, use a chain with links larger than the average commercially available bolt cutter. Also, heavy locks should be used; refrain from installing locks available at any convenience store. (Photos 7-1 and 7-2 show two examples of poor perimeter security taken from a major operator's tank farm in metropolitan Houston, Texas, 2002.)

Illumination/lighting is a simple but effective means to enhance perimeter control. To prove this to yourself, consider why most crimes occur at night.

The primary focus is to illuminate the area outside the fence to discourage approaching intruders. Also, provide lighting inside the fence directed towards the wellhead or building. Fixed installations such as refineries, tank farms, and loading docks normally have electrical power, which eases lighting installation. Remote sites may require installation of a small self-contained solar package similar to those used to power many signs and lights on road and freeway systems. Solar systems can effectively meet these requirements as energy efficient lighting technology has reduced power requirements significantly in recent years.

Motion detection and alarms. Unmanned sites can be equipped with electronic motion detection equipment. The two primary principles involve motion detection using a fixed light beam or a 'trembler' to identify motion in a fence or gate. Each can be adjusted to overlook movement by small animals. Sites in areas experiencing substantial wind disturbances may be restricted to the light beam technology.

Detection equipment can be designed for several purposes. The minimum design is to activate an audible or visual alarm to frighten the intruder sufficiently to cancel his mission. Loud sirens are effective. Rotating lights or strobe lights also cause panic. The systems can be conventionally powered or with a solar package. The detector can be rigged to a hidden camera to photograph the intruder at designated time frames.

Stand-alone systems may be used for remote well or unmanned offshore platforms. Larger installations usually deploy detection equipment linked to a monitoring system, whether actively or passively manned.

Video monitoring. Cameras provide video monitoring of the oil site. A simple camera system is designed to capture a photograph(s) or video when the detector is activated. Current digital models can store several thousand still photos or record hours of video without downloading. This approach is favored for remote wells and pipelines.

Cameras can be uplinked for satellite transmission to a receiver station. This affords greater storage capability or monitoring by security personnel. Uplink transmission technology is cost effective and can be designed with low power requirements.

Large installations require a dedicated multi-unit camera system with manned security. Signaling can be with coaxial cable or wireless technology. Camera site selection should cover heavy traffic areas and sections of the perimeter or facility that are difficult for the security team to monitor.

Cosmetic deterrence. In some cases, using dummy camera installations or posting warning signs that a camera is in use has proven as effective as live cameras in avoiding attacks. Consider installing non-functional rotating, colored, or strobe lights at installation corners. Additional signs can be displayed on the perimeter fence. Examples include:

- Guard Dog Patrolled
- Monitored by Surveillance Camera
- Security Personnel On Site
- Danger: Toxic Fumes
- Electric Fence

Clearly subordinate to functional security systems, cosmetic deterrence methods have excellent cost-benefit ratios.

Internal Control
Employee Management. Police force representatives indicate that a company's employees cause most problems at facilities. The individual employee may be disgruntled and cause the damage himself or collaborate with others to cause problems. Occasionally, employees will provide necessary intelligence to terrorists or other attackers either by deliberately selling or inadvertently revealing the information. Improving employment practices and providing employees with training about terrorists and their modus operandi reduces these situations. This has the added advantage of better equipping a company's employees to identify terrorists and other problem situations.

Identification. Consideration should be given to requiring employee IDs and two forms of photo IDs. The employee should carry them at all times. New technology imprints a digital photo into the ID material, which avoids the possibility that photos can be changed. Bar codes with a host of security and personal information also can be included. This allows electronic access where a manned system would otherwise be required. Also, the cardholder's access to various sections of the facilities can be controlled and monitored.

Finger printing. This method is an effective method to screen prospective employees or to police existing personnel if an incident occurs. History indicates this procedure culls terrorists and other undesirable individuals during the screening process when made aware that finger printing is required. Databases are available to perform background checks if desired. Note that requiring, obtaining, and using fingerprints by an employer is legal and common practice as long as the employee signs an appropriate waiver at the time of finger printing.

Credit checks. Running a credit check often provides unanticipated rewards. An individual claiming to have been unemployed for 6 months is unlikely to have a spotless credit report. Persons residing in the U.S. for extended time periods should have some credit history, if only for utility services such as telephone or electric service. Also, a troublemaker is less likely to pose as a potential employee if he is made aware that a credit check will be performed.

Reference Checks. Confirming references is a simple, effective security measure seldom practiced in employment assessment and control. Trained clerical staff performing this function can identify trouble signs. A prospective employee deemed to have fictitious work and personal references is unlikely to become the mainstay of a company's labor force.

SECURITY PERSONNEL

Although most oil and service companies have a security department and associated personnel, their staff size usually is insufficient to handle security needs at multiple sites. Third party companies and consultants are contracted to fill the void. Typically, off duty policemen and/or members of a security company are used.

Police. Police personnel offer an attractive option to satisfy part-time or special requirements. Although slightly more costly than typical security guards, police officers bring added dimensions to the security job. City and states usually license their officers with full police authorization on a 24-hour basis throughout their employment, even if the officer is not on active duty. Effectively, this means that an off duty officer working at a part-time security assignment has the same capabilities as if on duty police personnel were performing the task. The officer usually has received extensive training, often as much as 6-8 months initially with on-going training in areas of specialization. If an incident occurs where the police force becomes involved, an off duty officer working as a security guard may be able to mobilize the force, fire department, or emergency medical personnel more quickly than a security company's dispatcher. Also, off duty police officers frequently have more experience handling adverse situations.

Private Security. Specialized companies handle the bulk of security requirements. They provide required equipment and/or personnel as needed. Their personnel usually receive some training, perhaps up to three weeks in some cases. Attention must be given to selecting and monitoring a third party security company to guarantee vigilance on the job and that the personnel are qualified for the task.

As a cautionary final comment on this issue, consider that security personnel are commonly the lowest compensated employees at an oil installation, but these individuals enjoy protected freedom of access to most areas in the installation. Police departments report that many internal thefts are perpetrated by security personnel.

Canine Support. Special purpose dogs have become an integral part of security work. They serve several purposes including routine patrolling, intimidation, bomb and drug detection, and scent tracking. Often, the dog and its handler are considered as a single unit.

These dogs are not cross-trained for bomb and drug detection. Dogs with bomb training usually have scent tracking ability. Dogs for drug detection serve this single purpose. Both types are necessary for high-risk installations or in cases where drug issues are present.

SELECTING OPTIMUM SECURITY MEASURES

What are the best security measures for a given situation? Do we use the same level of security for all assets? How much is enough? The answers to these questions are important and necessary to develop an effective security program with the optimum value-for-money spent.

Guidelines for selecting oil site security measures are shown in Table 7-6. These guidelines provide a good foundation for most sites and serve as a reasonable starting point for a company to define their own requirements. Each company should review these guidelines against their own standards or special needs prior to implementation.

1-Category definitions from risk assessment:

L   Low risk
M   Medium risk
H   High risk
H_o High risk, optional

2-May vary depending on site, locale and company requirements

Table 7-6: Guidelines for Selecting Optimum Security Measures

Guidelines for Selecting Optimum Security Measures [1,2]										
Security Option	Well	Pipeline		Refinery	Offshore Structure		Storage Facility	Loading Terminal	Dock	Tank Farm
		exposed	pump		manned	unmanned				
Fence:										
standard	L,M	L,M	L,M	L			L	L	L	L
reinforced	H	H	H	M,H			M,H	M,H	M,H	M,H
Lights:										
standard	M		H	L		L,M	L	L	L	L
reinforced	H	H	H	M,H	L,M,H	H	M,H	M,H	M,H	M,H
Alarm:										
audible	H	H	H	L,M,H	L,M,H	L,M,H	L,M,H	L,M,H	L,M,H	L,M,H
visual	H	H	H	L,M,H	L,M,H	L,M,H	L,M,H	L,M,H	L,M,H	L,M,H
monitored	H	H	H	L,M,H	M,H	L,M,H	L,M,H	L,M,H	L,M,H	L,M,H
Manned:	H_0		H	H	H		L,M,H	L,M,H	L,M,H	L,M,H
Canine:										
drug				M,H	H_0		H	H	H	H
bomb				M,H	H_0		H	H	H	H
Patrol:										
car	H	H		M,H	L,M,H		L,M,H	L,M,H	L,M,H	L,M,H
boat					H_0	H_0		H_0	H_0	
air				H_0	H_0	H_0	H_0	H_0	H_0	H_0

TERRORIST THREAT CONDITIONS

Protection and security measures must be consistent with the potential threat. Although desirable to prepare for worst-case conditions, the practicality of maintaining a long term, high readiness level has not proven feasible. The better approach is for an expert group to establish various threat levels and determine the appropriate security measures that can be taken by the affected groups. Of course, the secret to success in this endeavor is to establish the proper threat levels.

The most widely recognized and accepted threat level definition has been established by the U.S. Department of Defense (DOD). Originally known as THREATCON, the name has recently been updated to Terrorist Force Protection Condition with the acronym, FPCON. The system uses progressive protection levels implemented in response to terrorist threats against U.S. personnel and facilities.

The FPCON is applicable for oil sites and operations. It covers these threat classes: (1) general nature, (2) marine, and (3) aviation. The five FPCON conditions and three classes contain numerous subdivisions covering most aspects of the oil industry. System adoption for oil operations is recommended as it places the industry in step with military operations for terrorism threat preparedness.

The system uses five protection condition groups. As specified by the DOD, they are as follows:

FPCON NORMAL: This condition exists when a general threat of possible terrorist activity exists but warrants only a routine security posture.

FPCON ALPHA: This condition applies when there is a general threat of possible terrorist activity against personnel and facilities, the nature and extent of which are unpredictable, and circumstances do not justify full implementation of FPCON BRAVO measures. However, it may be necessary to implement certain measures from higher FPCONS resulting from intelligence received or as a deterrent. The measures in this FPCON must be capable of being maintained indefinitely.

FPCON BRAVO: This condition applies when an increased and more predictable threat of terrorist activity exists. The measures in this FPCON must be capable of being maintained for weeks without causing undue hardship, affecting operational capability, and aggravating relations with local authorities.

FPCON CHARLIE: This condition applies when an incident occurs or intelligence is received that indicates some form of terrorist action against personnel and facilities are imminent. Implementation of measures in this FPCON for more than a short period probably will create hardship and affect the peacetime activities of the unit and its personnel.

FPCON DELTA: This condition applies in the immediate area where a terrorist attack has occurred or when intelligence has been received that terrorist action against a specific location or person is likely. Normally, this FPCON is declared for a localized condition.

The complete FPCON system with details is provided in Appendix A.

AFTERWORD

In my opinion, someone has needed to write this book for a long time. I have spent decades working for the oil industry, with companies that would fly me in with a jet and spend two million dollars to resolve a crisis situation. I've had many opportunities to get to know the issues of interdependence, oil manipulation, and the differences in perspective between the Western world and the rest of the globe. I knew the time would come when our oil dependence would be considered a critical target for attack.

Osama bin Laden, his followers, and other fundamentalist terrorism factions have nothing to lose and (in their view) everything to gain by planning and mounting future attacks. Much of bin Laden's wealth came from oil-related construction—he is now too rich to be touched. All he needs at this point is a couple of knowledgeable engineers and enough money to put the plan in action, and he can create a life-altering experience for much of the Western world.

My fear is that we have already forgotten the implications of 9/11 and will not understand the need for change until that life-altering experience has already occurred. The U. S. has become a "fat and lazy" society, accustomed to the idea of endless energy supplies far into future generations. But we don't understand how other parts of the world are viewing the situation.

As a world champion black-belt holder in karate, I've had the opportunity to train five young men for world championships. Time and again, I told them, "You have to stay hungry. It's the hungry competitor who has the drive to get to the top."

I think the U. S. has long lost that hunger and doesn't understand the ferocious drive of other factions to obtain world dominance through any means. If at times this book has seemed to dwell too heavily on U. S. issues, it is because the U. S. has become the world's greatest potential energy vulnerability. Disrupt our supplies, and watch the domino effect to the rest of the world.

We need to make every possible effort to remedy this situation, through increased domestic production, emphasis on development of significant alternative fuel sources, conservation, and a drastically revised domestic and global energy policy.

I hope someone is listening.

APPENDIX A

THREATCON SYSTEM

FAS Note: Pursuant to DOD Instruction 2000.16 dated 14 Jun 01, the term "Terrorist Threat Condition" (THREAT-CON) has now been replaced by the term "Terrorist Force Protection Condition" (FPCON). Individual classifications and measures remain the same.

SECTION I. BASIC THREATCON PROCEDURES

1. General. The threat conditions (THREATCONs) outlined below describe the progressive level of a terrorist threat to all US military facilities and personnel under DOD Directive O-2000.12. As approved by the Chairman of the Joint Chiefs of Staff, the terminology and definitions are recommended security measures designed to ease inter-Service coordination and support of US military antiterrorism activities. The purpose of the THREAT-CON system is accessibility to, and easy dissemination of, appropriate information. The declaration, reduction, and cancellation of THREATCONs remain the exclusive responsibility of the commanders specified in the order. Although there is no direct correlation between threat information (e.g., Intelligence Summaries, Warning Reports, and Spot Reports) and THREATCONs, such

information, coupled with the guidance provided below, assists commanders in making prudent THREATCON declarations. THREATCONs may also be suffixed with the geographic area deemed at risk. Once a THREATCON is declared, the selected security measures are implemented immediately. NOTE: When used in antiterrorism plans, recommend that the information contained in this appendix be marked "For Official Use Only" (FOUO) in accordance with DOD Regulation 5400.7-R, October 1990. The DOD Directive O-2000.12 recommended measures are:

THREATCON NORMAL exists when a general threat of possible terrorist activity exists but warrants only a routine security posture.

THREATCON ALPHA applies when there is a general threat of possible terrorist activity against personnel and facilities, the nature and extent of which are unpredictable, and circumstances do not justify full implementation of THREATCON BRAVO measures. However, it may be necessary to implement certain measures from higher THREATCONs resulting from intelligence received or as a deterrent. The measures in this THREATCON must be capable of being maintained indefinitely.

(1) Measure 1. At regular intervals, remind all personnel and dependents to be suspicious and inquisitive about strangers, particularly those carrying suitcases or other containers. Watch for unidentified vehicles on or in the vicinity of US installations. Watch for abandoned parcels or suitcases and any unusual activity.

(2) Measure 2. The duty officer or personnel with access to building plans as well as the plans for area evacuations must be available at all times. Key personnel should be able to seal off an area immediately. Key personnel required to implement security plans should be on-call and readily available.

(3) Measure 3. Secure buildings, rooms, and storage areas not in regular use.

(4) Measure 4. Increase security spot checks of vehicles and persons entering the installation and unclassified areas under the jurisdiction of the United States.

(5) Measure 5. Limit access points for vehicles and personnel commensurate with a reasonable flow of traffic.

(6) Measure 6. As a deterrent, apply measures 14, 15, 17, or 18 from THREATCON BRAVO either individually or in combination with each other.

(7) Measure 7. Review all plans, orders, personnel details, and logistic requirements related to the introduction of higher THREATCONs.

(8) Measure 8. Review and implement security measures for high-risk personnel as appropriate.

(9) Measure 9. As appropriate, consult local authorities on the threat and mutual antiterrorism measures.

(10) Measure 10. To be determined.

THREATCON BRAVO applies when an increased and more predictable threat of terrorist activity exists. The measures in this THREATCON must be capable of being maintained for weeks without causing undue hardship, affecting operational capability, and aggravating relations with local authorities.

(1) Measure 11. Repeat measure 1 and warn personnel of any other potential form of terrorist attack.

(2) Measure 12. Keep all personnel involved in implementing antiterrorist contingency plans on call.

(3) Measure 13. Check plans for implementation of the next THREAT-CON.

(4) Measure 14. Move cars and objects (e.g., crates, trash containers) at least 25 meters from buildings, particularly buildings of a sensitive or prestigious nature. Consider centralized parking.

(5) Measure 15. Secure and regularly inspect all buildings, rooms, and storage areas not in regular use.

(6) Measure 16. At the beginning and end of each workday, as well as at other regular and frequent intervals, inspect the interior and exterior of buildings in regular use for suspicious packages.

(7) Measure 17. Examine mail (above the regular examination process) for letter or parcel bombs.

(8) Measure 18. Check all deliveries to messes, clubs, etc. Advise dependents to check home deliveries.

(9) Measure 19. Increase surveillance of domestic accommodations, schools, messes, clubs, and other soft targets to improve deterrence and defense, and to build confidence among staff and dependents.

(10) Measure 20. Make staff and dependents aware of the general situation in order to stop rumors and prevent unnecessary alarm.

(11) Measure 21. At an early stage, inform members of local security committees of actions being taken. Explain reasons for actions.

(12) Measure 22. Physically inspect visitors and randomly inspect their suitcases, parcels, and other containers. Identify the visitor's destination. Ensure that proper dignity is maintained, and if possible, ensure that female visitors are inspected only by a female qualified to conduct physical inspections.

(13) Measure 23. Operate random patrols to check vehicles, people, and buildings.

(14) Measure 24. Protect off-base military personnel and military vehicles in accordance with prepared plans. Remind drivers to lock vehicles and check vehicles before entering or exiting the vehicle.

(15) Measure 25. Implement additional security measures for high-risk personnel as appropriate.

(16) Measure 26. Brief personnel who may augment guard forces on the use of deadly force. Ensure that there is no misunderstanding of these instructions.

(17) Measures 27. As appropriate, consult local authorities on the threat and mutual antiterrorism measures.

(18) Measures 28 and 29. To be determined.

THREATCON CHARLIE applies when an incident occurs or intelligence is received indicating some form of terrorist action against personnel and facilities is imminent. Implementation of measures in this THREATCON for more than a short period probably will create hardship and affect the peacetime activities of the unit and its personnel.

(1) Measure 30. Continue, or introduce, all measures listed in THREAT-CON BRAVO.

(2) Measure 31. Keep all personnel responsible for implementing antiterrorist plans at their places of duty.

(3) Measure 32. Limit access points to the absolute minimum.

(4) Measure 33. Strictly enforce control of entry. Randomly search vehicles.

(5) Measure 34. Enforce centralized parking of vehicles away from sensitive buildings.

(6) Measure 35. Issue weapons to guards. Local orders should include specific orders on issue of ammunition.

(7) Measure 36. Increase patrolling of the installation.

(8) Measure 37. Protect all designated vulnerable points. Give special attention to vulnerable points outside the military establishment.

(9) Measure 38. Erect barriers and obstacles to control traffic flow.

(10) Measure 39. Consult local authorities about closing public (and military) roads and facilities that might make sites more vulnerable to attacks.

(11) Measure 40. To be determined.

THREATCON DELTA applies in the immediate area where a terrorist attack has occurred or when intelligence has been received that terrorist action against a specific location or person is likely. Normally, this THREATCON is declared as a localized condition.

(1) Measure 41. Continue, or introduce, all measures listed for THREATCONs BRAVO and CHARLIE.

(2) Measure 42. Augment guards as necessary.

(3) Measure 43. Identify all vehicles within operational or mission-support areas.

(4) Measure 44. Search all vehicles and their contents before allowing entrance to the installation.

(5) Measure 45. Control access and implement positive identification of all personnel—no exceptions.

(6) Measure 46. Search all suitcases, briefcases, packages; etc., brought into the installation.

(7) Measure 47. Control access to all areas under the jurisdiction of the United States.

(8) Measure 48. Make frequent checks of the exterior of buildings and of parking areas.

(9) Measure 49. Minimize all administrative journeys and visits.

(10) Measure 50. Coordinate the possible closing of public and military roads and facilities with local authorities.

(11) Measure 51. To be determined.

SECTION II.
SHIPBOARD TERRORIST
THREAT CONDITIONS

2. Shipboard Terrorist THREATCON Measures. The measures outlined below are for use aboard vessels and serve two purposes. First, the crew is alerted, additional watches are created, and there is greater security. Second, these measures display the ship's resolve to prepare for and counter the terrorist threat. These actions will convey to anyone observing the ship's activities that the ship is prepared, the ship is an undesirable target, and the terrorist(s) should look elsewhere for a vulnerable target. The measures outlined below do not account for local conditions and regulations or current threat intelligence. The ship's command must maintain flexibility. As threat conditions change, the ship's crew must be prepared to take actions to counter the threat. When necessary, additional measures must be taken immediately. The simple solution to THREATCON CHARLIE or DELTA is to get under way, but this option may not always be available.

THREATCON ALPHA is declared when a general threat of possible terrorist activity is directed toward installations, vessels, and personnel, the nature and extent of which are unpredictable, and where circumstances do not justify full implementation of THREATCON BRAVO measures. However, it may be necessary to implement certain selected measures from THREATCON BRAVO as a result of intelligence received or as a deterrent. The measures in this threat condition must be capable of being maintained indefinitely.

(1) Measure 1. Brief crew on the threat, ship security, and security precautions to be taken while ashore.

(2) Measure 2. Muster and brief security personnel on the threat and rules of engagement.

(3) Measure 3. Review security plans and keep them available. Keep on call key personnel who may be needed to implement security measures.

(4) Measure 4. Consistent with local rules, regulations, and status of forces agreement, post qualified armed fantail sentry and forecastle sentry. Rifles are the preferred weapon.

(5) Measure 5. Consistent with local rules, regulations, and SOFA, post qualified armed pier sentry and pier entrance sentry.

(6) Measure 6. Issue two-way radios to all sentries, roving patrols, quarterdeck watch, and response force. If practical, all guards will be equipped with at least two systems of communication (e.g., two-way radio, telephone, whistle, or signal light).

(7) Measure 7. Issue night vision devices to selected posted security personnel.

(8) Measure 8. Coordinate pier and fleet landing security with collocated forces and local authorities. Identify anticipated needs for mutual support (security personnel, boats, and equipment) and define methods of activation and communication.

(9) Measure 9. Tighten shipboard and pier access control procedures. Positively identify all personnel entering pier and fleet landing area— no exceptions.

(10) Measure 10. Consistent with local rules, regulations, and SOFA, establish unloading zone(s) on the pier away from the ship.

(11) Measure 11. Deploy barriers to keep vehicles away from the ship. Barriers may be ship's vehicles, equipment, or items available locally.

(12) Measure 12. Post signs in local language(s) to explain visiting and loitering restrictions.

(13) Measure 13. Inspect all vehicles entering pier and check for unauthorized personnel, weapons, and/or explosives.

(14) Measure 14. Inspect all personnel, hand-carried items, and packages before they come aboard. Where possible, screening should be at the pier entrance or foot of brow.

(15) Measure 15. Direct departing and arriving liberty boats to make a security tour around the ship and give special attention to the waterline and hull. Boats must be identifiable night and day to ship's personnel.

(16) Measure 16. Water taxis, ferries, bum boats, and other harbor craft require special concern because they can serve as an ideal platform for terrorists. Unauthorized craft should be kept away from the ship; authorized craft should be carefully controlled, surveilled, and covered.

(17) Measure 17. Identify and inspect workboats.

(18) Measure 18. Secure spaces not in use.

(19) Measure 19. Regulate shipboard lighting to best meet the threat environment. Lighting should include illumination of the waterline.

(20) Measure 20. Rig hawsepipe covers and rat guards on all lines, cable, and hoses. Consider using an anchor collar.

(21) Measure 21. Raise accommodation ladders, stern gates, jacob ladders, etc., when not in use. Clear ship of all unnecessary stages, camels, barges, oil donuts, and lines.

(22) Measure 22. Conduct security drills to include bomb threat and repel boarders exercises.

(23) Measure 23. Review individual actions in THREATCON BRAVO for possible implementation.

(24) Measure 24. To be determined.

THREATCON BRAVO is declared when an increased and more predictable threat of terrorist activity exists. The measures in this THREATCON must be capable of being maintained for weeks without causing undue hardships, without affecting operational capability, and without aggravating relations with local authorities.

(1) Measure 25. Maintain appropriate THREATCON ALPHA measures.

(2) Measure 26. Review liberty policy in light of the threat and revise it as necessary to maintain the safety and security of the ship and crew.

(3) Measure 27. Conduct divisional quarters at foul weather parade to determine the status of on-board personnel and to disseminate information.

(4) Measure 28. Ensure that an up-to-date list of bilingual personnel for the area of operations is readily available. Ensure the warning tape in the pilot house and/or quarterdeck that warns small craft to remain clear is in both the local language and English.

(5) Measure 29. Remind all personnel to: (a) be suspicious and inquisitive of strangers, particularly those carrying suitcases or other containers; (b) be alert for abandoned parcels or suitcases; (c) be alert for unattended vehicles in the vicinity; (d) be wary of any unusual activities; and (e) notify the duty officer of anything suspicious.

(6) Measure 30. Remind personnel to lock their parked vehicles and to carefully check them before entering.

(7) Measure 31. Designate and brief picket boat crews. Prepare boats and place crews on 15-minute alert. If the situation warrants, make random picket boat patrols in the immediate vicinity of the ship with the motor whaleboat or gig. Boat crews will be armed with M16 rifles, one M60 with 200 rounds of ammunition, and 10 concussion grenades.

(8) Measure 32. Consistent with local rules, regulations, and SOFA, establish armed brow watch on pier to check identification and inspect baggage before personnel board ship.

(9) Measure 33. Man signal bridge or pilot house and ensure flares are available to ward off approaching craft.

(10) Measure 34. After working hours, place armed sentries on a superstructure level from which they can best cover areas about the ship.

(11) Measure 35. Arm all members of the quarterdeck watch and SAT. In the absence of a SAT, arm two members of the SDF.

(12) Measure 36. Provide shotgun and ammunition to quarterdeck. If the situation warrants, place sentry with shotgun inside the superstructure at a site from which the quarterdeck can be covered.

(13) Measure 37. Issue arms to selected qualified officers to include Command Duty Officer (CDO) and Assistant Command Duty Officer (ACDO).

(14) Measure 38. Arm Sounding and Security Patrol.

(15) Measure 39. Muster and brief ammunition bearers or messengers.

(16) Measure 40. Implement procedures for expedient issue of firearms and ammunition from small arms locker (SAL). Ensure a set of SAL keys are readily available and in the possession of an officer designated for this duty by the commanding officer.

(17) Measure 41. Load additional small arms magazines to ensure adequate supply for security personnel and response forces.

(18) Measure 42. Inform local authorities of actions taken as the THREATCON increases.

(19) Measure 43. Test communications with local authorities and other US Navy ships in port.

(20) Measure 44. Instruct watches to conduct frequent random searches under piers, with emphasis on potential hiding places, pier pilings, and floating debris.

(21) Measure 45. Conduct searches of the ship's hull and boats at intermittent intervals and immediately before it puts to sea.

(22) Measure 46. Move cars and objects such as crates and trash containers 100 feet from the ship.

(23) Measure 47. Hoist boats aboard when not in use.

(24) Measure 48. Terminate all public visits.

(25) Measure 49. Set materiel condition YOKE, main deck and below.

(26) Measure 50. After working hours, reduce entry points to the ship's interior by securing selected entrances from the inside.

(27) Measure 51. Duty department heads ensure all spaces not in regular use are secured and inspected periodically.

(28) Measure 52. If two brows are rigged, remove one of them.

(29) Measure 53. Maintain capability to get under way on short notice or as specified by SOP. Consider

possible relocation sites (different pier, anchorage, etc.). Rig brow and accommodation ladder for immediate raising or removal.

(30) Measure 54. Ensure .50-caliber mount assemblies are in place with ammunition in ready service lockers (.50-caliber machineguns will be maintained in the armory, prefire checks completed, and ready for use).

(31) Measure 55. Prepare fire hoses. Brief designated personnel on procedures for repelling boarders, small boats, and ultralight aircraft.

(32) Measure 56. Obstruct possible helicopter landing areas in such a manner as to prevent hostile helicopters from landing.

(33) Measure 57. Review riot and crowd control procedures, asylum-seeker procedures, and bomb threat procedures.

(34) Measure 58. Monitor local communications (e.g., ship-to-ship, TV, radio, police scanners).

(35) Measure 59. Implement additional security measures for high-risk personnel as appropriate.

(36) Measure 60. Review individual actions in THREATCON CHARLIE for possible implementation.

(37) Measures 61 and 62. To be determined.

THREATCON CHARLIE is declared when an incident occurs or intelligence is received indicating that some form of terrorist action against installations, vessels, or personnel is imminent. Implementation of this THREATCON for more than a short period will probably create hardship and will affect the peacetime activities of the ship and its personnel.

(1) Measure 63. Maintain appropriate measures for THREATCONs ALPHA and BRAVO.

(2) Measure 64. Cancel liberty. Execute emergency recall.

(3) Measure 65. Be prepared to get under way on one 1 hour's notice or less. If conditions warrant, request permission to sortie.

(4) Measure 66. Muster and arm SAT, BAF, and reserve force (RF). Position SAT and BAF at designated location(s). Deploy RF to protect command structure and augment posted security watches.

(5) Measure 67. Place armed sentries on a superstructure level from which they can best cover areas about the ship.

(6) Measure 68. Establish .50- or .30-caliber machinegun positions.

(7) Measure 69. If available, deploy STINGER surface-to-air missiles IAW established ROE.

(8) Measure 70. Energize radar and establish watch.

(9) Measure 71. Ships with high-power sonars operate actively for random periods to deter underwater activity. Man passive sonar capable of detecting boats, swimmers, or underwater vehicles. Position any non-sonar-equipped ships within the acoustic envelope of sonar-equipped ships.

(10) Measure 72. Man one or more repair lockers. Establish communications with an extra watch in DC Central.

(11) Measure 73. Deploy picket boat. Boats should be identifiable night and day from the ship (e.g., by lights or flags).

(12) Measure 74. If feasible, deploy a helicopter as an observation or gun platform. The helicopter should be identifiable night and day from the ship.

(13) Measure 75. Activate antiswimmer watch. (Portions of watch may already be implemented by previous THREATCON measures).

(14) Measure 76. Issue weapons to selected officers and chief petty officers in the duty section (i.e., the commanding officer, executive officer, department heads).

(15) Measure 77. Issue concussion grenades to topside rovers, forecastle and fantail sentries, and bridge watch.

(16) Measure 78. Erect barriers and obstacles as required to control traffic flow.

(17) Measure 79. Strictly enforce entry control procedures and searches—no exceptions.

(18) Measure 80. Enforce boat exclusion zone.

(19) Measure 81. Minimize all off-ship administrative trips.

(20) Measure 82. Discontinue contract work.

(21) Measure 83. Set materiel condition ZEBRA, second deck and below.

(22) Measure 84. Secure from the inside all unguarded entry points to the interior of the ship.

(23) Measure 85. Rotate screws and cycle rudder(s) at frequent and irregular intervals.

(24) Measure 86. Rig additional firehoses. Charge the firehoses when manned just prior to actual use.

(25) Measure 87. Review individual actions in THREATCON DELTA for implementation.

(26) Measure 88. To be determined.

THREATCON DELTA is declared when a terrorist attack has occurred in the immediate area or intelligence has been received that indicates a terrorist action against a specific location or person is likely. Normally, this THREATCON is declared as a localized warning.

(1) Measure 89. Maintain appropriate THREATCONs ALPHA, BRAVO, and CHARLIE measures.

(2) Measure 90. Permit only necessary personnel topside.

(3) Measure 91. Prepare to get under way and, if possible, cancel port visit and depart.

(4) Measure 92. Post sentries with M60 machinegun(s) to cover possible helicopter landing areas.

(5) Measure 93. Arm selected personnel of the SDF.

(6) Measure 94. Deploy M-79 grenade launchers to cover approaches to ship.

(7) Measure 95. To be determined.

SECTION III.
AVIATION FACILITY THREATCON PROCEDURES

3. General. In addition to basic THREATCON procedures, a variety of other tasks may need to be performed at aviation facilities. This is particularly true for airbases located in areas where the threat of terrorist attacks is high.

THREATCONs ALPHA AND BRAVO

(1) Planning

(a) Review THREATCONs ALPHA and BRAVO measures.

(b) Update THREATCONs ALPHA and BRAVO measures as required.

(2) Briefing and Liaison

(a) Brief all personnel on the threat, especially pilots, ground support crews, and air traffic controllers.

(b) Inform local police of the threat. Coordinate plans to safeguard aircraft flight paths into and out of air stations.

(c) Ensure duty officers are always available by telephone.

(d) Prepare to activate contingency plans and issue detailed air traffic control procedures if appropriate.

(e) Be prepared to receive and direct aircraft from other stations.

(3) Precautions Inside the Perimeter

(a) Perform thorough and regular inspection of areas within the perimeters from which attacks on aircraft can be made.

(b) Take action to ensure no extremists armed with surface-to-air missiles can operate against aircraft within the perimeter.

(c) Establish checkpoints at all entrances and inspect all passes and permits. Identify documents of individuals entering the area—no exceptions.

(d) Search all vehicles, briefcases, packages, etc., entering the area.

(e) Erect barriers around potential targets if at all possible.

(f) Maintain firefighting equipment and conduct practice drills.

(g) Hold practice alerts within the perimeter.

(4) Precautions Outside the Perimeter

(a) Conduct, with local police, regular inspections of the perimeter—especially the area adjacent to flight paths.

(b) Advise the local police of any areas outside the perimeter where attacks could be mounted and that cannot be avoided by aircraft on takeoff or landing.

(c) Advise aircrews to report any unusual activity near approach and over-shoot areas.

THREATCON CHARLIE

(1) Planning

(a) Review THREATCON CHARLIE measures.

(b) Update THREATCON CHARLIE measures as required.

(2) Briefing and Liaison

(a) Brief all personnel on the increased threat.

(b) Inform local police of increased threat.

(c) Coordinate with the local police on any precautionary measures taken outside the airfield's perimeters.

(d) Implement appropriate flying countermeasures specified in SOPs when directed by air traffic controllers.

(3) Precautions Inside the Perimeter

(a) Inspect all vehicles and buildings on a regular basis.

(b) Detail additional guards to be on call at short notice and consider augmenting firefighting details.

(c) Carry out random patrols within the airfield perimeter and maintain continuous observation of approach and overshoot areas.

(d) Reduce flying to essential operational flights only. Cease circuit flying if appropriate.

(e) Escort all visitors.

(f) Close relief landing grounds where appropriate.

(g) Check airfield diversion state.

(4) Precautions Outside the Perimeter

(a) Be prepared to react to requests for assistance.

(b) Provide troops to assist local police in searching for terrorists on approaches outside the perimeter of military airfields.

THREATCON DELTA

(1) Planning

(a) Review THREATCON DELTA measures.

(b) Update THREATCON DELTA measures as required.

(2) Briefings and Liaison

(a) Brief all personnel on the very high levels of threat.

(b) Inform local police of the increased threat.

(3) Precautions Inside the Perimeter

(a) Cease all flying except for specifically authorized operational sorties.

(b) Implement, if necessary, appropriate flying countermeasures.

(c) Be prepared to accept aircraft diverted from other stations.

(d) Be prepared to deploy light aircraft and helicopters for surveillance tasks or to move internal security forces.

(4) Precautions Outside the Perimeter. Close military roads allowing access to the airbase.

GLOSSARY

ANWR. Arctic National Wildlife Refuge

API. American Petroleum Institute

API gravity. An arbitrary scale expressing the gravity or density of liquid petroleum products.

alternative fuel capacity. The onsite ability to switch between and utilize two or more fuel sources.

bcf. Billions of standard cubic feet, generally of gas

barrel. A volumetric measure for crude oil and petroleum products equivalent to 42 US gallons.

basin. A geographic area in which sediments accumulate.

battery. The production handling equipment on a lease. Also called a tank battery.

bbl/ton. Barrels per ton

bit, drill. An attachment placed on the lower end of a drill string that cuts or grinds rock formations.

blowout. An uncontrolled flow of gas, oil, or other fluids from a well.

bomb. A container filled with an explosive, incendiary or other chemical for dropping or hurling, or for detonating with a timing mechanism.

bomb, dirty. A device using conventional explosives as a dispersing means for radioactive sources.

bomb, suicide. A bomb delivered by a human with death as a reasonably certain outcome upon detonation.

brine. Water with a large quantity of dissolved salt in it.

brisance. A measure of the shock effects produced by explosives.

btu. British thermal unit, a measure of heating value of a fuel

bulk terminal. A facility used primarily for the storage and/or marketing of petroleum products, which has a total storage capacity of 50,000 barrels or more and/or receives petroleum products by tanker, barge or pipeline.

C4. A malleable, highly stable explosive substance, usually off-white in color.

cartel. A combination of independent commercial or industrial enterprises designed to limit competition or fix prices.

casing. Steel pipe lowered in a well for protection from underground formations.

cell. Any of the smallest organizational units of a group or movement.

cement. A compound place around casing in oil wells to secure the casing and protect weak formations.

choke point. A location in oil and gas transport routes where flow could easily be disrupted.

christmas tree. Assembly of valves, pipe and fittings used to control flow of oil and gas from a well.

compressor station. An installation located on a pipeline system, which contain compressors to move natural gas through a pipeline.

condensate. Hydrocarbons which are in a gaseous state under reservoir conditions but which become liquid either in passage up the hole or in the surface equipment.

crude oil. A mixture of hydrocarbons that exists in the liquid phase in the underground reservoir and remains liquid at atmospheric pressure after passing through surface separation facilities.

dwt. Dead weight ton (dwt x 7.07 = bbls)

deliverability. Volume of gas that can be moved through a point in a pipeline grid system per day.

deliverability, storage. The amount of gas or oil that can be withdrawn daily from a storage system.

depletion. Removal of hydrocarbons from a reservoir, usually accompanied by a reduction in pressure.

detonator. A device required to initiate an explosion in some classes of highly brisant materials.

development well. A well drilled within the proved area of an oil or gas reservoir to the depth known to be productive.

disruption. A change in a normal flow or transportation schedule of oil or gas.

drilling fluid. Also called mud; a mixture of water or oil and chemicals used in the drilling process.

dual fuel. Having the ability to use two types of fuel for the same purpose.

EEC. European Economic Community

EIA. Energy Information Administration

enhanced oil recovery. Improved methods applied to a hydrocarbon reservoir to increase production.

exploration. Search for reservoirs containing hydrocarbons.

field. An area consisting of a single reservoir or multiple reservoirs all grouped on, or related to, the same individual geological structural feature or stratigraphic condition.

fluid. A substance that flows and can include liquids or gases.

fracturing. Application of hydraulic pressure to the reservoir formation to create fractures through which oil or gas may move to the wellbore.

gas, natural. A mixture of hydrocarbons with small quantities of various non-hydrocarbons existing in the gaseous phase.

gas, solution. Gas dissolved in oil. It evolves from the oil as pressure is reduced.

gas, sour. A gas containing elements of hydrogen sulfide, H2S

gas, sweet. A gas that does not contain hydrogen sulfide, H2S

gas-oil ratio. (GOR) The number of cubic feet of gas produced with a barrel of oil.

gathering lines. The flow lines which run from several wells to a central lease or plant facility. Also called gathering system.

giant. Reservoirs with more than 100 million recoverable barrels.

grid. A pipeline system with laterals or branches from the mainline that form a network.

hole, dry. A well that failed to produce commercial quantities of oil or gas.

hydrocarbon. A compound consisting of molecules of hydrogen and carbon. Petroleum is a mixture of hydrocarbons.

imports. Receipts of crude oil and petroleum products into one country from another country.

injected gas. High-pressure gas injected into a formation to maintain or restore pressure or otherwise enhance recovery.

interruptible service. A sales volume or pipeline capacity made available to a customer without a guarantee of delivery, usually at a lower cost per unit when service is available.

LNG. Liquefied natural gas. Natural gas that has been subjected to high pressures and low temperatures that causes the gas to condense into a liquid phase.

OCS. Outer Continental Shelf

OPEC. The acronym for the Organization of Petroleum Exporting Countries that have organized for the purpose of negotiating with oil companies on matters of oil production, prices and future concession rights. Current members are Algeria, Indonesia, Iran, Iraq, Kuwait, Libya, Nigeria, Qatar, Saudi Arabia, United Arab Emirates, and Venezuela. The Neutral Zone between Kuwait and Saudi Arabia is considered part of OPEC.

off-peak period. Period of low contract demand, such as summer months in northern climates.

perforating. Creating flow paths from the casing to rocks to allow hydrocarbon flow.

Persian Gulf. A body of water accessed via the Strait of Hormuz with contiguous countries of Bahrain, Iran, Iraq, Kuwait, Qatar, Saudi Arabia, and the United Arab Emirates.

Pipeline trunk. A long distance, large diameter pipeline that generally connects supply areas to end-market users.

Pipeline grid. A network of many interconnections and delivery points that operate in and serve major market areas.

reserves, possible. Unproved volume of reservoirs, which analysis of geologic and engineering data suggests are less likely to be recovered than probable reserves.

pressure maintenance. Maintaining reservoir pressure by injecting fluid, normally water or gas, or both.

primary recovery. The amount of oil or gas produced from a reservoir by the reservoir's natural sources of energy.

processing plant. A facility designed to recover natural gas liquids from the stream of natural gas and to control the quality of natural gas being marketed.

production. The yield of an oil well.

proven reserves. Oil or natural gas deposits considered as 90% likely to be producible.

producing platform. An offshore structure that accommodates a number of producing wells.

refinery. An installation that manufactures finished petroleum products from crude oil and other hydrocarbon sources.

reservoir. A subsurface porous and permeable rock body that contains oil, gas, or both.

rig. A collection of equipment including the derrick, draw works, and attendant surface equipment that performs drilling, completion, or workover operations, also a rotary rig.

sandstone. A compacted sedimentary rock composed of quartz or feldspar. It is a common rock in which petroleum and water accumulate.

Shihad. An individual performing a suicide bombing.

Strategic Petroleum Reserve. Petroleum products stored by the Federal Government as a safeguard against supply disruptions.

sour crude. Oil containing free sulphur or other sulphur compounds whose total sulphur content is in excess of 1%.

state-sponsored terrorism. A terrorist organization based in, supported by, and receiving some level of control and influence from that country's government.

stimulation. Utilizing procedures, equipment and/or chemicals to improve reservoir production

stock tank. A lease tank into which a well's production is run.

structure. An underground geological feature capable of forming a reservoir for oil and gas.

super giant. Reservoirs with more than 500 million recoverable barrels.

super tanker. A vessel with capacity greater than 25,000 dwt.

sweet. Oil or gas when it contains no sour impurities.

TAPS. Trans-Alaska Pipeline System

tcf. Trillion standard cubic feet, generally of gas

tank farm. An installation used by gathering companies, trunk pipeline companies, and others to store crude oil.

target, soft. Targets with low levels of security and easy access.

target, hard. Targets with high security levels and restricted access.

terrorism, state. A form of terrorism operating within a country that supports and directs terrorist activities.

terrorism, transnational. Terrorist operations existing in one or more governing entities, with or without the knowledge, consent or support of the particular governing body within that country.

trunkline. A long distance, large diameter pipeline system linking a major supply source with a major market area.

ULCC. A vessel with capacity greater than 320,000 dwt.

VLCC. A vessel with capacity of 160,000 – 319,999 dwt.

water drive. The reservoir drive mechanism whereby oil is produced by the expansion of the underlying water, which forces oil into the wellbore.

water flooding. A method of enhanced recovery in which water is injected into an oil reservoir to force additional oil out of the reservoir rock and into the well bores of producing wells.

well, delineation. Wells drilled at some distance from an exploratory well and used to identify the extent of the reservoir in the area.

well, depleted. A well in which all commercial quantities of oil or gas have been produced.

well, discovery. The initial well that proves the presence of oil and gas.

well, directional. A well where lower sections are deviated at angles above 3-40.

well, flowing. A well that produces without any means of artificial lift.

well, exploratory. A well drilled to find oil or gas in an unproven area.

well, horizontal. A well having a portion of its course path oriented at approximately 90° to upper wellbore sections.

well, infill. Wells drilled inside reservoir boundaries to increase produced quantities of oil or gas.

well, producer. A well producing commercial quantities of oil or gas.

well, relief. A well designed to intersect and control a blowout or an uncontrolled well.

wellhead. The equipment used on the well at ground level to maintain surface pressure control.

workboat. A boat or self-propelled barge used to carry supplies, tools, and equipment to a job site offshore.

REFERENCES

AUDIO BOOKS AND CDS

Carr, C. 2002. *The Lessons of Terror*. Simon & Schuster.

Crowther, D.S. 1996. *40 Keys to Family Emergency Readiness*. Horizon Publishers.

Miller, J., Engelberg, S., Broad, W. 2001. *Germs, Biological Weapons and America's Secret War*. Simon & Schuster.

21st Century Complete Guide to Bioterrorism, Biological and Chemical Weapons, Germ Warfare, Nuclear and Radiation Terrorism. U.S. Government Press.

21st Century Guide to First Response and Survival in Emergencies and Disasters. U.S. Government Press.

BOOKS

Executive Protection, Kidnapping

Adams, A. A. 1999. *Beware the Pale Horse*. Aegina Press, Inc.

Auerback, A.H. 1998. Ransom, *The Untold Story of International Kidnapping.* New York: Henry Holt and Company.

Danto, B. L. 1990. *Prime Target, Security Measures for the Executive at Home and Abroad.* The Charles Press.

Glazebrook, J., Nicholoson, L. 1994. *Executive Protection Specialist Handbook.* Kansas City: Varro Press.

Holder, P. T., Hawley, D. L. 1998. *The Executive Protection Professional's Manual.* Butterworth-Heinemann.

June, D. L. 1999. *Introduction to Executive Protection.* CRC Press.

Mares, B. 1994. *Executive Protection, A Professional's Guide to Bodyguarding.* Paladin Press.

Maurquez, G. G. 1997. *News of a Kidnapping.* New York: Alfred A. Knopf.

Pelton, R. Y. 1999. *Come Back Alive.* Doubleday.

Steele, P. 1992. *Kidnapping, Past and Present.* New Discovery Books.

Explosives & Weapons

Benson, R. 1990. *Modern Weapons Caching.* Paladin Press.

Davis, T. L. 1943. *The Chemistry of Powder & Explosives.* Angrief Press.

Howard, D.A. 1990. *The Survival Chemist.* Desert Publications.

McLean, D. 1992. *The Do-It-Yourself Gunpowder Cookbook.* Paladin Press.

McPherson, J. 1979. *Terrorist Explosives Handbook. Volume 1, The Irish Republican Army.* Lancer Militia.

Pickett, M. 1999. *Explosives Identification Guide.* Delman Publishers.

Wells, R. 1984. *The Anarchist Handbook, Volumes 1, 2 and 3*. Desert Publications.

U.S. Government. 1992. *Explosives and Demolitions*. Dept. of the Army.

First Responder Chem-Bio Handbook, Practical Manual for First Responders. Tempest Publishing. 1998.

U.S. Government. 1974. *U.S. Navy Seal Combat Manual*. Dept. of the Navy.

Two Component High Explosives Mixtures. Desert Publications, 1982.

Improvised Shaped Charges. Desert Publications, 1982.

Royal Engineer's Handbook. Desert Publications, 1977.

Improved Munitions Black Book. Desert Publications, 1978.

Evaluation of Improvised Shaped Charges. Desert Publications, 1980.

Improvised Munitions Handbook, Volume 1 and 2. Desert Publications.

CIA, Field Expedient Incendiary Manual. Desert Publications, 1977.

General Terrorism

Anderson, S. K., Sloan, S. 2002. *Historical Dictionary of Terrorism*. The Scarecrow Press Inc.

Cronon, I. 2002. *Confronting Fear, A History of Terrorism*. Thunder's Mouth Press.

Heuvel, K. V. 2002. *A Just Response*. Thunder's Mouth Press/ Nation Books.

Hudson, R. A. 1999. *Who Becomes a Terrorist and Why, The 1999 Government Report on Profiling Terrorists*. The Lyons Press.

Ide, A. F., Auliff, J. R. 2002. *Jihad, Mujahideen, Taliban, Usama bin Laden, George W. Bush & Oil; A Study in the Evolution of Terrorism & Islam.* Tanglewuld Press.

Katz, S. 2002. *Relentless Pursuit, The DSS and the Manhunt for The Al-Qaeda Terrorists.* Tom Doherty Associates, LLC.

Laqueur, W. 1999. *The New Terrorism.* Oxford University Press.

Netanyahu, B. 2001. *Fighting Terrorism.* Farrar, Straus and Giroux.

Osterholm, M. T., Schwartz, J. 2000. *Living Terrors, What America Needs to Know to Survive the Coming Bioterrorist Catastrophe.* Dell Publishing.

Prados, J. 2002. *America Confronts Terrorism.* Ivan R. Dee Publishing.

Reich, W. 1990. *Origins of Terrorism.* The Woodrow Wilson Center Press.

Samenow, S.E. 1984. *Inside the Criminal Mind.* Crown Business.

Schweitzer, G. E. 2002. *A Faceless Enemy.* Perseus Publishing.

Stern, J. 1999. *The Ultimate Terrorists.* Harvard University Press.

Frequently Asked Questions about the Earth Liberation Front. 2001. North American Elf Press Office.

Petroleum

Economides, M. J., Oligney, R. 2000. *The Color of Oil.* Round Oak Publishing.

Introduction to Oil and Gas Production. 1996. American Petroleum Institute.

Security

Amend, K.K., Ruiz, M. S. *Hand Writing Analysis.* New Page Books.

Anderson, R. 2001. *Security Engineering, A Guide to Building Dependable Distributed Systems.* Wiley Computer Publishing.

Vohryzek-Bolden, M., Olson-Raymer, G., Whamond, J. O. 2001. *Domestic Terrorism and Incident Management.* Charles Thomas Publisher, Ltd.

Bevelacqua, A., Stilp, R. 2002. *Terrorism Handbook for Operational Responders.* Delmar Publishers.

Broder, J. F. 2000. *Risk Analysis and the Security Survey.* Butterworth-Heinemann.

Broussard, P.A. 1994. *Energy Security for Industrial Facilities.* Tulsa: PennWell Publishing Company.

Buck, G. 2002. *Preparing for Terrorism, An Emergency Services Guide.* Delmar Publishers.

Cumming, N. 1992. *Security, A Guide to Security System Design and Equipment Selection and Installation, 2nd Edition.* Butterworth-Heinemann.

Gagnon, R. M. 1998. *Design of Special Hazard & Fire Alarms.* Delmar Publishers.

Garcia, M. L. 2001. *The Design and Evaluation of Physical Protection Systems.* Butterworth Heinemann.

George, C., George, L. 1998. *Bomb Detection Dogs.* Capstone Books.

Kruegle, H. 1995. CCTV *Surveillance.* Butterworth-Heinemann.

Levitt, A.M. 1997. *Disaster Planning and Recovery.* John Wiley & Sons, Inc.

Maniscalco, P. M., Christen, H. T. 2002. *Understanding Terrorism and Managing the Consequences.* Prentice-Hall.

McCrie, R.D. 2001. *Security Operations Management.* Butterworth-Heinemann.

Mullen, S. 1994. *Emergency Planning Guide for Utilities.* Tulsa: PennWell Publishing Company.

Myers, K. N. 1999. *Contingency Planning for Disasters, 2nd Edition.* John Wiley & Sons, Inc.

Sennewald, C.A. 1998. *Effective Security Management, 3rd Edition.* Butterworth-Heinemann.

Related Subjects

Stiglitz, J. E. 2002. *Globalization And Its Discontents.* W.W. Norton & Company.

First Responder, 3rd Edition. American Academy of Orthopedic Surgeons, 2001

ARTICLES AND DOCUMENTS

Executive Protection & Kidnapping

Borger, J., Hooper, J. *"Evidence of six hijacking teams,"* www.guardian.co.uk, Oct. 12, 2001.

Vialls, J. *"HOME RUN; Electronically Hijacking the World Trade Center Attack Aircraft,"* www.homerun.com, Oct. 2001.

"Another oil worker killed in Lagos," www.oilandgasinternational.com, Dec. 17, 2001.

"Anthrax found at BP Petco Office," www.oilandgasinternational.com, Nov. 8, 2001.

"Colombia–National Liberation Army (NLA), or *Ejercito de Liberacion Nacional (ELN),"* www.dos.gov, 1999.

"EXECUTIVE PROTECTION," www.nancyhighshoe.com, 1997.

"*ExxonMobil field in Aceh bombed,*" www.oilandgasinternational.com, Dec. 12, 2001.

"*Hijackings,*" www.aviationsafetynetwork.org, 2002

"*It can't happen to me,*" www.consultgreen.com, 2001

"*One killed near Indonesia's Aceh gas fields,*" www.biz.yahoo.com, Dec. 21, 2001.

"*Plane Presumed down carrying 8 oil execs to Algeria,*" www.oil andgasinternational.com, Oct. 11, 2001.

"*Private oil & gas security info center revealed,*" www.oilandgasinter national.com, Dec. 9, 2001.

"*UK oil worker killed in Nigeria,*" www.oilandgasinternational.com, Nov. 28, 2001.

"*US offshore security tightening,*" www.oilandgasinternational.com, Dec. 15, 2001.

General Terrorism

Corsun, A. 1995. *Significant Incidents of Political Violence Against Americans.* U.S. Department of State.

Corsun, A. 1996. *Significant Incidents of Political Violence Against Americans.* U.S. Department of State.

Corsun, A. 1997. *Significant Incidents of Political Violence Against Americans, 10th Anniversary Issue.* U.S. Department of State.

Devost, M. G., Houghton, B. K. Pollard, N. A. 1996. "*Information Terrorism: Can You Trust Your Toaster?*" www.terrorism.com.

Franz, D. 2000. "*Agricultural Bioterrorism.*" Fifth Annual Emergency Preparedness Satellite Seminar Conference sponsored by the USDA, (September).

Ganor, B. 1998. *"Countering State-Sponsored Terrorism."* www.ict.com (April).

Ganor, B. 1997. *"Defining Terrorism: Is One Man's Terrorist Another Man's Freedom Fighter?"* www.ict.com.

Ganor, B. 2001. *"Terrorism: No Prohibition Without Definition."* www.ict.com (October).

Herren, E. *"Counter-Terrorism Dilemmas."* www.ict.com, April, 2002.

Herren, E. 1999. *"Information Processing in Counter-Terrorism."* www.ict.com (January).

Huxsoll, D. 2000. *"Agricultural Counterterrorism."* Fifth Annual Emergency Preparedness Satellite Seminar Conference sponsored by the USDA (September).

Johnson, D. 2001. *"Terrorist Attacks on Americans."* www.info-please.com/psot/terrorism6.html.

Karmon, E. 1998. *"Intelligence and the Challenge of Terrorism in the 21st Century."* www.ict.com (November).

Kohnen, A. 2000. *"Responding to the Threat of Agroterrorism: Specific Recommendations for the United States Department of Agriculture."* Harvard's Belfer Center for Science and International Affairs (October).

Paz, R. 2000. *"Targeting Terrorist Financing in the Middle East."* *www.ict.com* (October).

Rand, B. H. 1993. *"'Holy Terror' 1: The Implications of Terrorism Motivated By A Religious Imperative."* www.rand.org.

Shahar, Y. 2001. *"Tracing bin Laden's Money: Easier said than done."* www.ict.com (September).

Sloan, S. 1995. *"Terrorism: How Vulnerable Is The United States."* www.terrorism.com/terrorism/sloan.shtml (May).

"Al-Qaeda Manual." Al-Qaeda organization.

"*ATF Online.*" The Bureau of Alcohol, Tobacco and Firearms website download, www.atf.treas.gov.

"*BACKGROUNDER: TERRORISM.*"   www.fema.gov/old97/ terror.html, August, 1996.

"*Contending With Terror: Psychological Aspects.*" www.ict.com, June, 1997.

"*Countering the Changing Threat of International Terrorism: Report of the National Commission on Terrorism (for the 105th Congress).*" www.fas.org/irp/threat/commission.html, 2000.

"*Diary of Actions & Chronology.*" www.earthliberationfront.com, 2001.

"*FACT SHEET: TERRORISM.*" www.fema.gov/old97/terrorf.html, 1997.

"*FSK: Special Commando of the Defense.*" www.terrorism.com/ terrorism/FSK.shtml, 2000.

"*Frequently Asked Questions About Terrorism.*" www.terrorism. com/FAQ.shtml, 2000.

"*Global Trends 2015: A Dialogue About the Future with Nongovernment Experts.*" www.cia/gov. December, 2000.

"*Terrorism—Preparing for the Unexpected.*" www.redcross.org/ services/disaster/keepsafe/unexpected.html , 2002.

"*Terrorist Group Profiles.*" www.terrorism.com/terrorism/Groups2.shtml, 2000.

Petroleum

Alex, A. 2000. "*Risk of Infrastructure Failure in the Natural Gas Industry.*" PPT for Society of Risk Analysis (December).

Baker III, J. A. 1998. *"Unlocking the Assets: Energy and the Future of Central Asia and the Caucus—Main Study."* Houston: James A. Baker III Institute for Public Policy, Rice University (April).

Baud, R.D., et al. 2002. *Deepwater Gulf of Mexico 2002: America's Expanding Frontier.* Minerals Management Service.

Cook, J. S., Shirkey, C. P. 1989. *"A Review of Valdez Oil Spill Market Impacts."* www.eia.doe.gov (March).

Economides, M. J. *"Natural Gas Engineering, Energy Geopolitics."* Houston: PPT presentation, University of Houston.

Economides, M. J., Demarchos, A. S., Saputelli, L. 2002. *"Energy Sources and Energy Intensity for the Twenty-First Century."* SPE 77736.

Greene, D. L., Jones, D. W., Leiby, P.N. 1995. *"The Outlook For U.S. Oil Dependence."* U.S. Department of Energy.

Leiby, P.N., Jones, D. W., Curlee, T. R., Lee, R. 1997. *"Oil Imports: An Assessment of Benefits and Costs."* U.S. Department of Energy.

Johnson, D. 2002. *"Projects in the Pipeline."* www.infoplease.com/spot/caspianoil2.html (April).

Jones, D. W., Bjornstad, D. J., Leiby, P.N. 1997. *"The Findings of the DOE Workshop on Economic Vulnerability to Oil Price Shocks: Summary and Integration with Previous Knowledge, 2nd Draft."* U.S. Department of Energy.

Jones, D. W., Leiby, P.N. 1996. *"The Macroeconomic Impacts of Oil Price Shocks, A Review of Literature and Assets."* U.S. Department of Energy.

Karmon, E. 2002. *"The Risk of Terrorism against Oil and Gas Pipelines in Central Asia."* www.ict.com (January).

Kendell, J. K. 1998. *"Measures of Oil Import Dependence."* www.eia.doe.gov/oiaf/archive/issues98/oimport.html (July).

Klare, M. T. 2001. *"What bin Laden and Bush Don't Talk About: The Politics of Oil."* www.alternet.org/story.html (November).

Leiby, P.N., Jones, D. W., Curlee, T. R., Lee, R. 1997. *"Oil Imports: An Assessment of Benefits and Costs."* U.S. Department of Energy.

Noer, J. H. 1996. *"Southeast Asia Chokepoints, Keeping Sea Lines of Communication Open."* www.ndu.edu/inss/strforum/forum98.html (December).

Oligney, R. E., Economides, M. J. 2002. *"Natural Gas: The Excruciating Transition."* SPE 77371.

Riva, J.P. 1995. *"World Oil Production After Year 2000: Business as Usual or Crises?"* info@NCSEonline.org (August).

Thompson, J. M. 1997. *"U.S. Underground Storage of Natural Gas in 1997: Existing and Proposed."* Energy Information Administration/ Natural Gas Monthly (September).

"25th Anniversary of the 1973 Oil Embargo." www.eia.doe.gov/emeu/ 25opec/. 1999

"Alyeska Pipeline Service Company." www.alyeska-pipe.com (March, 2000.).

"Anti Terrorism Legislation: Iran Foreign Oil Sanctions Act Action Needed in Aftermath of Terrorism in Israel." www.bnaibrith.org/ pan/bombing.html (March, 1996.).

"Ashland Oil Spill." www.epa.doe.gov (March, 1999).

"Colonial Pipeline Spill." www.epa.doe.gov (March, 1999).

"Chronology of World Oil Market Events, 1970-2000." www.eia.doe. gov/emeu/cabs.chron.html (January, 2002).

"Deliverability on the Interstate Natural Gas Pipeline System." U.S. Department of Energy, 1998

"Emergency Response Notification System (ERNS)." www.epa.gov/ERNS (August, 2002).

"Fuel Oil Use in Manufacturing." www.eia.doe.gov/emeu/ consumptionbriefs/mecs/mecs_fueloil_use.html (May, 2002).

"High Prices Hurt Poor Countries More Than Rich." www.iea.org/
new/releases/2000/oilprice.htm (March, 2000).

"Impact of Interruptible Natural Gas Service on Northeast Heating Oil
Demand." U.S. Department of Energy, 2001.

"Iran-Iraq War." www.i-cias.com/e.o/iranirqw.html (April, 2002).

"Naval Petroleum Reserves." www.fe.doe.gov.

"Northeast Home Heating Oil Reserve." www.fe.doe.gov (August, 2001).

"Office of Pipeline Safety, Distribution Pipeline, Incident Summary by
Cause, 1/1/2001-12/31/2001." www.ops.dot.gov.stats/NGDIST01.HT
(March, 2002).

"Office of Pipeline Safety, Hazardous Liquid Pipeline, Accident
Summary by Commodity, 1/1/2001-12/31/2001." www.ops.dot.
gov.stats/LQ01_CM.HT (March, 2002).

"Office of Pipeline Safety, Natural Gas Transmission Pipeline Annual
Mileage." www.ops.dot.gov.stats (March, 2002).

"Office of Pipeline Safety, Transmission Pipeline, Incident Summary by
Cause, 1/1/2001-12/31/2001," www.ops.dot.gov.stats/NGDIST01.
HTM (March, 2002).

Offshore Technology Roadmap for the Ultra Deepwater Gulf of
Mexico. U.S. Department of Energy, 2000.

Oil and Gas Resources of the West Siberian Basin, Russia. U.S. Department of Energy, 1997.

"Oil Market Disruptions & Vulnerability." www.eia.doe.gov/security/
contingency.html (March, 2002).

"Oil Price Impacts on the U.S. Economy." www.eia.doe.gov/security/
sld001-005.html (January, 2000).

"Oil Production Capacity Expansion Costs For The Persian Gulf."
www.eia.doe.gov/TR/0606 (January, 1996).

"OPEC Bulletin." *Vol. XXXIII,* Nov. 4, 2002. www.opec.org (April, 2002).

"OPEC Fact Sheet." www.eia.doe.gov/emeu/cabs/opec.html (April, 2002).

"Petroleum: An Energy Profile, 1999." U.S. Department of Energy, 1999.

"Petroleum Reserves." www.fossilenergy.gov, 2002.

"Pipeline." www.infoplease.com/ipd/A0589985.html, April, 2002.

"Potential Oil Production from the Coastal Plain of the Arctic National Wildlife Refuge: Update Assessment." U.S. Department of Energy, 2000.

"Residential Heating Oil Prices: What Consumers Should Know." www.eia.doe.gov/oil_gas/petroleum/special/heating_update_update .html (February, 2002.).

"Responding to Spills." www.epa/gov/oilspill/response.htm (December, 1999).

"Rules-of-Thumb for Oil Supply Disruptions." www.eia.doe.gov.emeu/ cabs/rules.html (February, 2000).

"Strategic Petroleum Reserve." www.fe.doe.gov/spr/spr_facts.html (April, 2002).

"Strategic Petroleum Reserve—Quick Facts." www.fe.doe.gov.

"Tampa Bay Spill." www.epa.doe.gov/oilspill/tampabay.htm (March, 1999).

"The Effect of the National Security of Imports of Crude Oil and Refined Petroleum Products." U.S. Department of Commerce. 1999.

"The Effects of the Alaska Oil and Natural Gas Provisions of H.R. 4 and S. 1766 on U.S. Energy Markets." Department of Energy, 2002.

"The Trans Alaska Pipeline System (TAPS)." www.ndo.ak.blm.gov2000, 2000.

"United Nations Office of the Iraq Programme, Oil for Food." www.un.org/Depts/oip/ (January, 2000.).

"United Nations Office of the Iraq Programme, Implementation of Oil-for-Food—A Chronology." www.un.org.Depts/oip/chron.html (February, 2002).

"World Energy "Areas to Watch." www.eia.doe.gov/emeu/security/hot.html (August, 2001)

"World Oil Market and Oil Price Chronologies: 1970-2001." www.eia.doe.gov/emeu/cabs/chron.html (January, 2002).

"World Oil Transit Chokepoints." www.eia.doe.gov/cabs/choke.html (November).

Related Subjects

Brain, M. 2002. *"If daytime running lights were mandatory in the U.S., and all vehicles had them, how much extra gasoline would that use each year?"* www.howstuffworks.com.

Camp, J. 1995. *"Terror in the Heartland."* www.cnn.com (May 5, 1995).

Christensen, J. 1999. *"Bracing for guerrilla warfare in cyberspace."* www.cnn.com (April 6, 1999).

Collins, B.C. 1996. *"The Future of CyberTerrorism: Where the Physical and Virtual Worlds Converge."* www.acsp.uic.edu/OICJ/CONFS.

Condiotti, S. 1995. *"A painful decision."* www.cnn.com (May 9, 1995).

Condiotti, S. 1995. *"Federal Building Demolition."* www.cnn.com (May 23, 1995).

Oligney, R. E., Economides, M. J., Dunn, N. 2002. *Energy Integration.* Round Oak Publishing, In Press.

Pollard, N. A. 2000. *"The Future of Terrorism."* www.terrorism.com/terrorism/future.shtml.

Pollitt, M. M. 1997. *"CYBERTERRORISM–Fact or Fancy?"* www.fbi.gov.

Sproles, J., Byars, W. 1998. *"Cyber-terrorism."* www.ETSU.

Vesilind, P. J. 2002. *"Sixty years after Japanese bombers sank the U.S.S. Arizona, the silent wreck still sheds fuel oil, drop by drop, over the memories of a hellish Hawaiian morning."* www.nationalgeo graphic.com.

2002. *"Japanese Note to the United States December 7, 1941."* www.theavalonproject.com. Dept. of State Bulletin, Vol. V, No. 129, Dec. 13, 1941.

2002. *"Pearl Harbor."* www.encarta.msn.com.

2002. *"Pearl Harbor, Hawaii, Sunday, December 7, 1941."* www.THE-HISTORYPLACE/WorldWarTwoinEurope.com.

2002. *"PORTS, STRAITS, & NARROW CHANNELS."* www.turkishpilots.org/LINKS/LINKPORTS.HTML.

"The Bombing." www.cnn.com.

Security & Response

Borum, R., Fein, R., Vossekuil, B., Berglund, J. 1999. *Threat Assessment: Defining an Approach for Evaluating Risk of Targeted Violence, Behavioral Sciences and the Law.* John Wiley & Sons, Ltd.

Dunham, S. 2002. *"Mass Transit Defends Itself Against Terrorism."* Journal of Homeland Security. April, 2002.

Fein, R. A., Vossekuil, B. 1998. *"Protective Intelligence & Threat Assessment Investigations."* U.S. Department of Justice (July).

Fein, R. A., Vossekuil, B., Holden, G. 1998. *"Threat Assessment: An Approach To Prevent Targeted Violence."* National Institute of Justice, U.S. Department of Justice (July).

Lukaszewski, J. E., Cotton, M. A. N. 2002. *"First Response."* The Lukaszewski Group.

Porteus, L. 2002. *"Homeland security depends on new technologies, Ridge says."* National Journal's Technology Daily (April).

"911 Dispatch Monthly." www.911dispacth.com/911_file/911 explain.html (June, 2002).

"Awareness of National Security Issues and Response (ANSIR): FBI's National Security Awareness Program." www.fbi.gov.hq/nsd/ansir/ansir.htm (April, 1998).

"Early Warning Timely Response; A Guide to Safe Schools." www.ed.gov/offices/OSERS/OSEP/earlywrn.html (August, 1998).

"Emergency Contact Directory." www.fema.gov, 2002.

"Emergency Management Incident Checklist." www.fema.gov.

"FEMA Organization Chart." www.fema.gov/about/femaorg.shtm, 2002.

"Guide for All-Hazard Emergency Operations Planning." Federal Emergency Management Agency, (September, 1996).

"Public Awareness Advisory." Police Department, University of Minnesota, July, 2002.

"Relevant Security Resources on the Internet for Terrorism, Disaster Recovery and Related Subjects." www.asisonline.org/irc/html (March, 2002).

"USPS Messages to Customers: We Are Taking Every Possible Measure to Assure Safety of Customers and The Mail." www.usps.com/news/2991/press/pr01_1010tips.htm, 2001.

"United States Government Interagency Domestic Terrorism, Concept of Operations Plan." www.doj.gov. 1995.

Weapons and Explosives

DiZinno, J. A. *"Forensic Analysis of the Letter (from the 2001 Anthrax attacks)."* www.fbi.gov.

Ellis, R. W. 2000. *"Black Powder and How To Make It."* www.black-powdernet.com.

Fauci, A. 2002. *"An Expanded Biodefense Role for the National Institute of Health."* Journal of Homeland Security (April).

Gaunt, D. L., Kornguth, S.E. 2001. *"The University of Texas Biological and Chemical Countermeasures Program."* Journal of Homeland Security (September).

Helm, L. 2000. *Anarchy Cookbook Version 2000.*

Inglesby, T. V. et al. 1999. *"Anthrax as a Biological Weapon, A Consensus Statement."* Journal of the American Medical Association. May 12, 1999.

Jernigan, J. A. et al. 2001. *"Bioterrorism-Related Inhalational Anthrax: The First 10 Cases Reported in the United States."* Center for Disease Control and Prevention report published in Emerging Infectious Diseases. November-December, 2001.

Karmon, E. 2001. *"Are the Palestinians Considering Biological Weapons?"* ICT. August, 2001.

Karmon, E. 2001. *"The Anthrax Campaign, An Interim Analysis."* ICT. October, 2001.

Kramer, D.A. 2000. *Explosives.* U.S. Geological Survey Minerals Handbook.

Mueller, R. S. 2001. *"Anthrax Update."* www.fbi.gov. FBI news release, October 16, 2001.

Riley, M. *"Killer gave Internet advice on how to make explosives."* www.theage.com.au/news/2000/12/29/FFXIC7TA9HC.html (December, 2000).

"Biological and Chemical Terrorism: Strategic Plan for Preparedness and Response." Center for Disease Control and Prevention. www.cdc.gov/mmwr (April, 2000).

"Bomb-making instructions." www.CypherpunkHyperArchive.com, 1997.

"Bomb and Physical Security Planning." Bureau of Alcohol, Tobacco and Firearms, U.S. Department of the Treasury, 1987.

"Chemical/Biological/Radiological Incident Handbook" www.odci. gov/cia/publications/cbr_handbook/ (October, 1998).

"Country Analysis Briefs." www.eia.doe.gov and CIA country maps at www.lib.utexas.edu/maps/ for Angola, Azerbaijan, Caspian Region, Chechnya, China, Germany, Iran, Iraq, Kuwait, Malacca Straits, Malaysia, North Sea, Norway, Oman, Panama, Russia, South China Sea, Spratly Islands, Strait of Hormuz, Saudi Arabia, Singapore, Suez Canal, Turkey, United Kingdom, Yemen.

"Domestic Preparedness Program In The Defense Against Weapons of Mass Destruction." U.S. Department of Defense (May, 1997).

"Explosives, Bombs, Fireworks." www.sonic.net/~brucel/, 2002.

"Federal Officials Announce Anthrax Vaccine Policy." U.S. Department of Defense news release, June 28, 2002.

"Laboratory Chemical Hygiene Plan." MGH Research Affairs and MGH Safety Office.

"Linguistic and Behavioral Assessments of the Person Responsible for Mailing Anthrax-laden Letters on September 18 and October 9, 2001." Amerithrax Press Briefing, November, 2001. www.fbi.gov, 2001.

"Morbidity and Mortality Weekly Report." Center for Disease Control and Prevention. November 16, 2001.

"Protecting Buildings from Bomb Damage: Transfer of Blast Effects Mitigation Technologies from Military to Civilian Applications,

Commission on Engineering and Technical Systems, 1994."
www.nap.edu/openbook

"The Terrorist's Handbook." www.capricorn.org/~akira/home/terror.html.

"Terrorist Incident Planning Guidelines." Federal Emergency Management Agency. www.fema.gov. May, 2001.

"Unclassified Report to Congress on the Acquisition of Technology Relating to Weapons of Mass Destruction and Advanced Conventional Munitions." Director of Central Intelligence (DCI)." www.odci/gov/cia/publications, 1997.

INDEX

A

O

Osama bin Laden, 96, 99, 147
Outer Continental Shelf, 39-40

P

Pacific Ocean, 70
Pakistan, 91-92, 95
Panama Canal/Panama Pipeline, 45, 70-72
Pathogens, 96-99
Perimeter control/fences, 137-139
Persian Gulf, 43-44, 57, 60, 72, 92
Personnel (security), 141-142: police, 141-142; private security, 142; canine support, 142
Pesticides, 96, 100
Petrochemicals, 2-3
Petroleum books/articles/documents, 178, 183-188
Petroleum reserves (U.S.), 39-41: oil, 39-40; gas, 40-41
Petroleum reserves, 29, 37-41, 66, 102-103: world, 37-39; U.S., 39-41
Philippines, 70
Pipe bombs, 86
Pipeline risk assessment, 131
Pipelines, 23-24, 67-68, 106-113, 115, 120, 122, 131: proposals, 67-68; gas, 106-113; oil, 115; risk assessment, 131
Plague, 97
Poison gases/solids/liquids, 100
Police personnel, 141-142
Policy implications, 147-148
Political stability issues, 68
Pollution effect, 126-127
Polychlorinated biphenyls, 100
Port facility, 120, 124
Port of Ceyhan, 8, 67-68, 75
Port of Valdez, 23, 57, 59
Port of Yanbu, 60, 68
Price of oil, 45, 47-53
Primary explosives/initiators, 82
Private security personnel, 141-142
Process interruption (oil as target), 102
Production and unused capacity (oil), 43-45
Production facilities (offshore), 25-26
Propellants/low explosives, 82
Protection need determination, 134-136
Prudhoe Bay Field, 39
Psychology of fear, 79

S

T

V

W

Y